# These Signs Shall Follow Them That Believe

*Graced to be an instrument for Him*

Mary L. Daniel-Fuller

**author**HOUSE®

*AuthorHouse™*
*1663 Liberty Drive*
*Bloomington, IN 47403*
*www.authorhouse.com*
*Phone: 833-262-8899*

*Published by AuthorHouse   10/24/2023*

*ISBN: 979-8-8230-1548-6 (sc)*
*ISBN: 979-8-8230-1547-9 (e)*

*Library of Congress Control Number: 2023918620*

*Print information available on the last page.*

# CONTENTS

NEW YORK
- *Charge of negligence manslaughter dropped*
- *Woman healed from excruciating pain*
- *Phone shattered in pieces*
- *God's will trumps ours*
- *Lady delivered from abominable lifestyle*

# FOREWORD

Overseer Mary Daniel-Fuller is a dynamic woman of God and I've had the honor of knowing her for over a decade. I have watched my spiritual daughter grow as an energetic pastor, mother, chaplain, and, most of all, a woman of great faith. I have personally witnessed the impact of Overseer Mary Daniel-Fuller's ministry on several occasions. She has preached, taught, and brought numerous people through deliverance and restoration. Her delivery is second to none. Many times, I have watched the anointing of the Holy Ghost flow powerfully through her as healing power was released in room after room - a healing power that I felt in my own life. Every time I fellowship with her, the impact on my life is innumerable. Every moment has been therapeutic, phenomenal, and dynamic.

This book "These Signs Shall Follow Them That Believe! Graced To Be Used As An Instrument For Him" is one example of the fruit of Overseer Mary Daniel-Fuller's deliverance ministry. Each page will give you, the reader, practical examples of exercising your faith in the all-powerful and miraculous name of Jesus. It will not only enhance and uplift your faith, but it will also give you instructions to follow so you will believe in God. If you follow these instructions, you too can experience healing, deliverance, and restoration in the name of Jesus.

If you are reading this and have not purchased this book, you must get a copy! If you have, find a cozy location, read, and absorb every page! It will be a blessing to you.

*Evangelist Paulette P. Faulknor*
*Co-Pastor, First United Tabernacle International Ministry*
*Orange, New Jersey*

# ACKNOWLEDGEMENTS

I give honor to my Lord and Savior Jesus Christ, the Almighty God for the grace that He has placed over my life to give birth to this book – "These Signs Shall Follow Them That Believe ~ Graced To Be An Instrument For Him." The journey has been very long, but through God's timing and for His glory, these divine encounters and miracles are documented as proof that God still performs miracles.

To my dear miracle children – Rachel and Isaiah. You are my greatest joy and motivation, and I am forever grateful for the smiles, laughter, and inspiration you bring into my life. Thank you for sharing your Mommy on so many occasions.

Isaiah this book was conceived because of your inquisitive mind surrounding the things of God. You wanted the details of every assignment and because of that I began to document each miracle and divine encounter. You have been the driving force behind my writing.

Rachel my darling thanks for being a voice that speaks as a mouthpiece directly from God. You made it clear that without a shadow of a doubt that God has called me and so you will be there to support me in every aspect so that the perfect will of God can be fulfilled in my life. I love and appreciate you both.

Evangelist Dr. Sandra Bailey, I love, value, and admire you. Words cannot express how grateful I am for you. You stepped into God's divine order for my life to allow my dream to become a reality. Your dedication, prayers, and commitment prove that God still allows destiny helpers to work and assist in fulfilling the goals of others. You took this on like your own and I am honored to have had the opportunity to learn from you.

A heartfelt gratitude to you Evangelist Dr. Sharon Maylor. You are truly a gem. You gave of yourself without reservation, bringing ideas that made this project easier. God knows what He was doing when we met at that Women's Retreat, and you sat at the table and as the ideas were pouring out, you took your pen and wrote as God would have it to be so. I love you.

To my sister/mommy Donna, I love and treasure you for being there for me over the years, like a true sister should and at times playing the role of a mommy. When days are long and night seems endless you are always there as a voice that echoes, "You are cut out for this." Thank you, my Sister!

To my Daddy Albert Daniel, you are one of a kind, I cannot say it enough how much I love and respect you. You have been a tower of strength to me. Some of my siblings may say that I am spoiled, but you often would remind me because I was so sick as a child you had to keep a special pair of eyes out for me. Daddy, you are that kind of father that any girl would love to have growing up.

To my church family, New Apostolic International Ministries and the ministerial staff, thanks for your support during the times that I could not physically be on the prayer conference line. Your prayers and support are noticeable and appreciated, and you will be rewarded by our Heavenly Father. My chief armor bearer Missionary Harrington, my little sister in Christ Sister Kadian Lewis, Minister Hunter, my deepest gratitude for stepping into roles that helped me to fulfill God's calling on my life. To every parishioner of N-AIM thanks for allowing me to pour into your lives on a daily basis. I love you!

To all my friends, family members, mentors, Pastors, and Bishops who have been there for me over the years I thank you for believing in me. Your prayers, support, and your love I will forever hold dear to my heart.

To my dear Co-Pastor Paulette Faulknor thank you for being my spiritual mother and agreeing to write the forward for this book. You are a living testimony, proving once again that our God is a healer, and that He still works miracles.

Finally, I want to express my gratitude to all the readers who will embark on this literary journey. It is my sincere hope that this book resonates with you, touches your heart, and leaves a lasting impact. May your faith be strengthened as you take your time to read about the miracles and divine encounters, my prayer is that you also will experience God in a very supernatural way.

# DEDICATION

## *In loving memory of Ruby Ferrigon*

To my dear mother Ruby, to be absent in the body is to be present with the Lord. Though I cannot physically hand you a copy of this book, I know that you are with me, celebrating this achievement from beyond the realms of this world. Your love and spirit continue to inspire me every day, reminding me to embrace my creativity, persevere through challenges, and honor your legacy.

Your constant reminder that I am a very special child as always kept me going even though I was the seventh of ten siblings. This was not to discount my siblings; you saw in me what I did not see in myself. You were my biggest support in my personal life and ministry. You believed in my dreams even when I doubted myself, and your gentle words of wisdom, "Mary, you were born for a purpose." This pushed me forward during moments of self-doubt.

There are days I wish you were here in the physical, but I know you are looking down on me. You have left your signature mark in so many ways and deeds in my life and that of others. Your faith in God will forever motivate me to walk in my God given purpose. Sleep on mommy you are forever in my heart, and I will see you in the rapture.

# INTRODUCTION

*Miracles still happen and encounters can still be experienced!*

There is often talk in our world that miracles are a thing of the past. With the rise of knowledge, advancement in medicine, rise of technology and artificial intelligence, individuals believe that there is nothing known as a miracle. They feel that there is a scientific or logical explanation for everything that happens. However, a miracle is inexplicable by natural or scientific laws. The purpose of this book is to share through inspirational true stories that God continues to actively work miracles and change lives in a supernatural way. Despite what skeptics may say, God's power is still at work in the world today. It is also my hope that through the timely reading of this book, the faith of the believer will be strengthened, and conviction will come to the heart of unbelievers. The details of these powerful testimonies of God's miraculous intervention includes physical and spiritual healing, provisions made, divine supernatural encounters and answered prayers in the lives of ordinary people from all walks of life that I have personally witnessed.

I am humbled and in awe of the grace of God upon my life. His undeserved favor has allowed me to be a conduit through which His miraculous power continues to manifest. In this 21ˢᵗ century God has allowed me to live out *Mark 16: 17 – 18*, ***"And these signs shall follow them that believe; In my name shall they cast out devils; they shall speak with new tongues; They shall take up serpents; and if they drink any deadly thing, it shall not hurt them; they shall lay hands on the sick, and they shall recover."*** Miracles still happen and God has been using me to be a blessing to the Body of Christ and to bring His name glory. Coupled with the miracles, I am also the recipient of many divine encounters that have left me speechless and transformed. Above everything else these encounters have left me with an insatiable desire to know God MORE.

According to the Webster's dictionary the definition of a miracle is:

- A surprising and welcoming event not explainable by natural or scientific laws and is therefore considered the work of a Divine agency.
- It is an extraordinary event taken as a sign of the supernatural power of God, an extremely outstanding or unusual event, thing, or accomplishment.

Since Webster's dictionary outlines a miracle as an outstanding or unusual event, thing, or accomplishment, it is reasonable to say that we must employ our faith for us to see these miracles. According to *Hebrews 11:1*, **"Faith assures us of things we expect and convinces us of the existence of things we cannot see."** God has unlimited power, but it pleases Him to exercise His power in response to our faith. Jesus did not force divine blessings on people who openly rejected Him. He often performed miracles for those who already believed, and sometimes His miracles led to faith in those who did not previously believe (*St. John 11:45; 12:9 – 11; 14:11*). But Jesus would not perform miracles simply for His own personal benefit, it was to bring His Father glory and to make believers of unbelievers.

Our faith must be actively engaged for miracles to happen. In *St. Mark 6:5*, it states that Jesus could not work any miracles in His hometown because of their unbelief. It is much easier for one to hold on to something when it is tangible, but it is going to take faith to believe God for the intangible. Miracles are NOT magic but rather they are demonstrations of the power of God. There are at least three biblical tests for recognizing a legitimate miracle:

## 1. THE MIRACLE GLORIFIES GOD

Miracles declare that God is active in our world, and He can disrupt the activities of nature to reveal His character and accomplish His purposes. The principal test of a miracle is: Who receives the glory? Beware of people (such as Simon the sorcerer in *Acts 8:9*) who boast of their own greatness. When the children of Israel crossed the Red Sea on dry land; a miracle of no mean order, they glorified God. *Exodus 15: 1 – 25* records the song of praise and thanksgiving that they offered up to God for His miraculous doing.

## 2. THE MIRACLE STEMS FROM A RIGHTEOUS SOURCE

Jesus said that in the last days false prophets will come and perform great signs and wonders to deceive, if possible, even the very elect (*St. Matthew 24:24*). Someone's words may sound true, and their actions may be impressive, but they are counterfeit if their lives show no good fruit. Magic, spells, enchantments, sorcery, witchcraft, psychics, and wizardry are not miracles. Research has shown that occult magic is often a fraudulent and deceitful illusion — counterfeit miracles. Occult magic or divination are a manifestation of demonic powers or the result of demon possession (*Acts 16:16*). Of course, the power of Satan and his demons is extremely limited compared to God's power.

Those who follow the path of the magic arts are on the wrong path - a road that leads away from God, not toward Him. In one way or another, the end will be disastrous. The evil Queen Jezebel practiced witchcraft (*2 Kings 9:22*) bringing catastrophe on herself and all Israel. Over and over, God denounces those who "conjure spells" and those who practice witchcraft and sorcery. The Bible says that anyone who does these things is detestable to the Lord (*Deuteronomy 18:10-12*).

## 3. THE MIRACLE RINGS TRUE TO THE HOLY SPIRIT

According to Paul, one of the gifts of the Holy Spirit is distinguishing between spirits (*1 Corinthians 12:10*). Paul demonstrated this gift when he told Elymas, a Jewish sorcerer, that he was a child of the devil and an enemy of everything that is right (*Acts 13:10*). Through the Holy Spirit, Paul perceived the utter baseness that was in the man. Likewise, we must look to the Holy Spirit for guidance regarding the source of a miracle. Remember not everyone that says, Lord, Lord is of the kingdom of God.

The Bible records 120 miracles, most of them in the Old Testament. The four Gospels record 37 miracles of Jesus, who performed them as signs of His identity and authority. The New Testament reminds us also that Christ and His Apostles (through the power of the Holy Spirit) offered not merely "signs" of God's power, but what were described repeatedly as "signs and wonders" (*St. Matthew 24:24; St. Mark 13:22; St. John 4:48; Acts 4:30, 5:12, 14:3, 15:12; Romans 15:19; 2 Corinthians 12:12, 2 Thessalonians 2:9 and Hebrews 2:4*).

Let us look at some of the miracles in the Acts of the Apostles:

- *Acts 5:15*: Peter is so filled with the Holy Spirit that even his shadow has the power to heal, a fact that makes Groundhog Day even less impressive.
- *Acts 8:39*: after teaching about Christ and baptizing the Ethiopian eunuch, the Holy Spirit snatched Philip immediately in a scene almost reminiscent of Star Trek.
- *Acts 20:9-12*: a young man named Eutychus falls asleep and to his death out a third story window in the middle of Paul's preaching and later Paul brings him back to life.
- *Acts 28:3-6*: a poisonous viper sprung out of a campfire and latched onto Apostle's Paul's arm, only to be thrust off with Paul suffering no harm. The witnesses then thought Paul was a god.

In addition to all of these, the Apostles were witnessed healing the blind (*9:17-18*), the paralyzed (*9:33-35*), the lame (*14:7-9*), the possessed (*16:16-18*), and even a man with severe diarrhea (*28:7-8*) . . . you see, the Bible has everything!

Acts of the Apostles also has three dramatic jailbreaks (5:17-25; 12:5-11; 16:25-30), the divinely inspired rushing mighty wind at Pentecost (*2:2-6*), healing relics (*19:11-12*) and a worship service so powerful that the earth quaked (*4:31*)! During all these powerful acts of the Apostles, however, we cannot forget the formula. The Apostles do not perform miracles by their own power or for their own glory. The Apostles performed miracles only through the power of Jesus' name, directing all praise and glory to the risen Lord! Miracles, signs, and wonders did not stop with the Apostles, but it continues today with those who will believe! A promise was made that these signs shall follow them that believe.

Not all miracles happen the same way because our God is Sovereign and does what He wants, and when He wants, and how He wants. Miracles at times can be either performed:

## 1. IMMEDIATELY

Jesus was in the synagogue on the Sabbath and there was a man there who had a shriveled hand. All eyes were on Jesus... would He heal? After all, it was the Sabbath and performing a miracle was a form of work and working on the Sabbath was against customs and laws! The Pharisees were ready to pounce if Jesus even thought about healing that man. Not on the Sabbath... not on their watch! But Jesus always elevated people above procedures so He said to the man, "Stretch out your hand." So, he stretched it out and it was completely restored, just like the other one," (*St. Matthew 12:13*).

It was an immediate miracle, an instant healing. The man stretched his hand toward Jesus and Jesus made it whole! Some healings are like that. Instant. Unexplainable. When you least expect it. But, when God chooses to heal immediately, it is ultimately to glorify Himself. Healing proves He is Lord over the rules of man. He is bigger than our expectations! He is The One who chooses the time, the place and the way healing occurs. So, if you are longing for a miracle, stay in His presence and trust His timing. The account of the woman with the issue of blood recorded in *St. Luke 8: 43 – 48* as she touched the hem of His garment the Bible stated that immediately the flow of blood stopped that she was dealing with for twelve years.

## 2. GRADUALLY

Jesus and His disciples were going through Bethsaida, when some folks brought a blind man to Him asking for healing (*St. Mark 8:22-25*).

Jesus took the blind man by the hand, led him outside the village, and touched his eyes. Jesus asked, "Do you see anything?" The blind man looked up and squinted through a foggy haze and said, "I see people; they look like trees walking around." Things were still blurry. His sight was not totally restored.

Jesus did not heal him immediately, He could have, but He did not. Instead, He performed a gradual miracle. "Once more Jesus put his hands on the man's eyes. Then his eyes were opened, his sight was restored, and he saw everything clearly." The result was healing. The process was different because it was gradual, but the result was healing. Does that mean that gradual healing is like getting short-changed? Is it like getting a miracle from the clearance rack?

No, gradual healing is still healing, and we do not always understand why Jesus chooses to heal that way. But to me, gradual healing seems even more special because that blind man got to feel the touch of Jesus twice. The real blessing of healing is not only the result, but also the process. It is in the blessing that comes from being with Jesus, feeling His touch, His comfort, His presence. So, if "people still look like trees," if you have not received the full healing or miracle that you want, keep trusting God and thank Him for the honor of His continued presence and touch in your life. Remember He wants to make you whole, and His presence is far more satisfying than healing.

## 3. EVENTUALLY

The Apostle Paul had issues to deal with too. He had something painful in his life – he called it a thorn in the flesh; a messenger of Satan to buffet him. He asked God over and over to remove it, but God did not remove it during Paul's lifetime (*2 Corinthians 12:7-9*). As far as we know, Paul died with that painful thorn wedged in his soul. When God answered Paul's urgent plea for healing, God's response was not "no." I think His response was "not yet." Healing would come. God would answer Paul's prayer and the answer would come eventually just not now and not yet.

If God did not heal you yet, do not assume His answer is "no," His best answer for you may be "not yet, child." When God does not grant immediate or gradual thorn removal, He gives something far better, He gives Grace. That's what God gave to Paul, *"But He told me my kindness is all you need. My power is strongest when you are weak. So, I will brag even more about my weaknesses in order that Christ power will live in me,"* (2 *Corinthians 12:9*). Paul lived with his thorn, and he walked by faith through every question and every unmet longing. Eventually, Paul's faith became sight, and the thorn was removed for there are no thorns in heaven.

## SIGNS AND WONDERS

In the context of the Bible, "signs and wonders" refer to miraculous events that are believed to be evidence of God's power and presence. These events are often seen as supernatural occurrences that defy explanation by natural laws and are therefore attributed to divine agency. Examples of signs and wonders in the Bible include the plagues of Egypt during the Exodus, the parting of the Red Sea, the healing of the sick and disabled, and the resurrection of Jesus Christ. In each of these cases, the miraculous event was seen as a sign of God's power and a confirmation of His message or mission.

The story found in *2 Kings 5* speaks about a man called Naaman; a man of high degree. He was captain, honorable and a mighty man of valor yet he was stricken with leprosy. In the Bible, Naaman is described as a commander of the army of the king of Aram (Syria), who was afflicted with leprosy. Leprosy was a serious and contagious skin disease that was considered a curse from God in ancient times. It caused disfigurement, loss of sensation, and often led to social isolation and rejection.

He found out from a little slave girl who was his wife's maiden, that the Israelite prophet Elisha could heal him. Naaman responded pleasantly to her recommendation and went to see the prophet. According to science leprosy was an incurable disease yet through the voice of the prophet Elisha Naaman was completed healed. Naaman however had to follow direct instructions before he could receive his healing. The instruction was to go wash in Jordan River seven times; this was not what he was expecting. He thought he would have received an immediate miracle from the prophet. Jordan was not the best river and so Naaman was upset because he wanted to dictate how he should receive his healing. He stated, *"The Abana and Pharpar Rivers in Damascus have better water than any of the rivers in Israel. "Couldn't I wash in them and be clean? So, he turned around and left in anger,"* (2 *Kings 5:12*).

Naaman's miracle indicates that some miracles are done gradually and that one must follow the instructions given. He did not receive his miracle on the first, second or fifth time but on the seventh time as he was instructed. The miracle took place when the instructions were followed as given. The Bible states that on the seventh dip his skin became healthy again like a little child's skin. For us to experience and see the miracles of God we must STOP, TURN and LISTEN! This goes for the individual that is being a conduit for the miracle and the person who needs the miracle. Elisha had to tell Naaman exactly what God said and Naaman had to do exactly what the prophet instructed.

## STOP

To stop means to come to an end, cease to continue or cease to happen. Our God needs us to understand that for us to truly be an instrument to be used by Him, we must be able to stop doing what we want to do and be fully engaged to what He is about to say. God wants our complete attention as the Psalmist declares in *Psalm 46:10* that we should be still and know that He is God. We should be willing to let go of our cares, concerns, and past experiences so we can hear what the Lord wants to say to us. I encourage you to push the pause button and wait to see what the Lord has in store for you.

## TURN

Now that we have stopped going in our direction and our own way, if God is going to use us and if we are going to be recipient of His miracles and divine encounters then we must turn. To turn is to change direction when moving. God now wants us to go in the direction that He will point us in. Naaman had to turn in his mind and then in his actions. Even though he was angry with the prophets' directives he had to stop and turn to go in the direction of Jordan River to get his miracle. A turned mind without follow through actions will eventually result in doubt. Actions without a turned mind will eventually cause one to return to previous behaviors. Turning one's mind and aligning the actions to a turned mind go hand in hand.

## LISTEN

To listen is to pay keen attention to what is being said. Listening is very important to an individual who is graced to be an instrument for God's purpose. Oftentimes we miss important and valuable information because we fail to listen. Listening is the key to unlocking and doing great exploits for God. We must focus and pay attention to the one that is speaking so that we can have clarity concerning the instructions that are being given. Most of us, at some point in our lives can relate to the fact of missing one or more of these steps. The consequences showed itself in various ways like setbacks, delays, pain, heartaches and missed opportunities to name a few. *Ephesians 3:20*, **"Glory belongs to God, whose power is at work in us. By this power he can do infinitely more than we can ask or imagine."** We must understand that there is power in us, but we must follow a prescribed method to be the benefactor of His miracles.

I often remind myself according to *St. Mark 10:27*, **"It's impossible for people to save themselves, but it's not impossible for God to save them. Everything is possible for God."** Remember the story with the woman that had the issue of blood. She was sick for twelve years. She spent all that she had and was left with no cure and no hope; but she heard that Jesus was passing. She stopped, turned, and listened. She heard for sure that Jesus was passing by and most of all she believed that by His grace all things are possible. To truly come to full grip of the signs and wonders of God we must be at the place where we allow Him to be the dominant one in the relationship. According to *Proverbs*

*3:5-6, "Trust the Lord with all your heart, and do not rely on your own understanding. In all your ways acknowledge him, and he will make your paths smooth."* He needs to be intimate with us so that He can trust us enough with whatever He commands and demands. He needs that whenever He gives direct instructions, we will be in position to stop, turn and listen. I agree some things just does not make sense to the natural man but remember what He said in *1 Corinthians 1: 24 – 25, "But to those Jews and Greeks who are called, He is Christ, God's power, and God's wisdom. God's nonsense is wiser than human wisdom, and God's weakness is stronger than human strength."* We will have to trust Him because He has proven Himself that He never changes and that He is sovereign in all things.

His methods and styles may differ but that will never change His plans or purpose for our lives. No one ever said that trusting God was ever easy, but with faith as an accompaniment we will be able. Faith tells us that He is and that He is a rewarder to them that diligently seek Him. We should solely depend on Him even when there is nothing to trace Him. Simply trust Him. *Romans 11:33* declares, *"God's riches, wisdom, and knowledge are so deep that it is impossible to explain His decisions or to understand His ways."*

## DIVINE ENCOUNTERS

Divine encounters typically refer to experiences in which a person feels that they have had a direct, personal interaction with God. These encounters may take many forms, such as a vision, a voice, a feeling of overwhelming presence, or other mystical experiences. These are usually transformative experiences that can have a profound impact on a person's beliefs, values, and sense of purpose. Divine encounters are deeply personal and subjective experiences. They can occur during prayer, meditation, times of need or crisis, in nature. The experience is different for each person. People often report physical and emotional sensations during divine encounters - a feeling of profound peace, unconditional love, oneness with all creation, etc. The encounter can feel quite miraculous, inspiring awe and gratitude, a time when divinity meets humanity.

The phrase "graced to be used by Him" typically refers to the idea that someone feels blessed or honored to be used as an instrument or vessel for God's purposes. In this context, "Him" refers to God. To be "graced" means to be given a gift or blessing that is not deserved or earned. It implies that the person recognizes that their abilities and opportunities to serve God are not solely due to their own efforts or merits, but rather a result of God's grace and favor.

I have been graced by God to be used and witnessed many miracles and several divine encounters. These have left me feeling extremely privileged and blessed to know that God has chosen to grace me with such experiences. Each time they occur my desire to see and know more of God becomes heightened. Journey with me through these pages as I share with you the opportunities I have experienced being used as an instrument of grace.

# CHAPTER ONE

## HOW IT ALL BEGAN I AM A MIRACLE GRACED TO BE USED!

*"Before I formed you in the womb, I knew you. Before you were born, I set you apart for my holy purpose. I appointed you to be a prophet to the nations." - Jeremiah 1:5*

Every one of us is born for a purpose, whatever reason that is. Rest assure that our God is deliberate, and He is also purposeful. God did not create us to do nothing. His Word declares that we are a chosen people, a royal priesthood, a holy nation, people who belong to God. ***"You were chosen to tell about the excellent qualities of God, who called you out of darkness into His marvelous light,"*** (*1 Peter 2:9*). My life from what I can recall was never easy; but one thing for sure I am graced to be used by Him.

My late mother, Ruby would often remind me of the miracles and the miraculous power of the sovereign God over my life. My name was not randomly given by my Mom but by my late aunt, Mother Mary Bailey. My Mom would often say, "Mary you are a special child, I know you may be the seventh of ten children but remember what I say, you are very, very special." She would also remind me that I should have been dead, and would say often, "Mary oh Mary you are a special child, and a special girl." Whenever she had an opportunity to talk about her ten children, she would say it took a miracle for me to be alive because of the circumstances that surrounded my birth. I was born prematurely in the island of Jamaica in the city of Kingston.

Welcoming yet another child who would become the seventh of ten children she handled and cared for me extra special because of the uniqueness of my birth. Upon arriving home, Mom decided to make sure that no mosquitoes, flies, or bugs got close to my crib. Like any good mother she would lite a mosquito repellant and put it directly where my crib was to prevent mosquitoes from biting me. One day after a few hours of leaving me in my crib to do her house chores she came to check on me. Mom said she found me blue, pale, and with not much life. She screamed and screamed to get my father's attention; for at this point, I was not breathing. My Dad then told my Mom, "Let's go." Upon arriving at the University Hospital, my Mom recalled doctors and medical staff attempting to bring me back to life. Mom said that after a few attempts one doctor told her to put the child down because I was dead.

The doctor was unaware of the fact that my Mom who had already been blessed with six children was NOT going to let go of this her special child called, Mary. Mom placed me on the bed that they had provided, and she kept praying and believing God for a miracle. She was believing Him for the supernatural. They covered my small body with a white sheet but even with that Mom kept praying. Mom knew that the effectual fervent prayers of the righteous avails much and that the God she served still works miracles. She was holding on to her faith. After everyone had cleared the room, she stood over my lifeless body and prayed her last prayer, "God I will dedicate Mary to you if you would return life back in her body."

The miraculous happened and I am still here today. The power of God's miraculous grace showed up. Mom with her eyes closed heard a male voice saying, "Mother, Mother look, look! Something is moving under the sheet." My tiny feet were moving up and down. The voice was from a young resident doctor that was going about his business when he heard the prayers of my Mom and paused to show reverence to what he was hearing. Not only did he hear my Mother's prayers, but he got to witness and experience the miraculous power of grace. God granted my Mom her request and she was able to take me home. Do not forget that miracles happen every day. According to *Jeremiah 32:27* **"I am the Lord God of all humanity. Nothing is too hard for me."**

Indeed, as humans we fail at times to believe that God can do all things but fail. Do not forget that God's Word is true. Do not forget that purpose cannot die; destiny must be fulfilled. I have come to the realization and acceptance that God has a way of fulfilling every word that has been spoken over our lives. God's ways are not our ways, neither His thoughts our thoughts. When my Mother dedicated my life to God it meant serving Him and being used as an instrument for Him. This is where it all began, being dead; no life; except for the prayer of a committed, dedicated and believing Mother. God showed up and showed off. That day God magnified Himself to all that stood around. *Psalm 77:14* states, **"You are the God who performs miracles. You have made your strength known among the nations."** Today, God continues to show the doctors, clinicians, and those around that He is all powerful and mighty and He continues to perform wonders every day.

## THE PREPARATION PROCESS

I migrated to the United States of America at the age of seventeen and resided in the state of Florida. Many told me that this was the land of opportunities. It was said that it is the Big Apple and so it is waiting for me to "bite off" a piece. There was so much unsolicited advice. I was told that I could be whatever I wanted to be; however, the struggles were real. Living with my brothers and sisters coming from the island I was bouncing from one apartment to another. My Mom would do live - in jobs to make sure we were comfortable. She also took odd jobs to keep afloat.

Different lifestyles were knocking hard at my door that would have provided me with money and the promise of a famous life. However, the only thing that was pressing me after seeing the good versus the evil was to continue in the things that I had learned. I was baptized and filled with the Holy Ghost and was a member of a small assembly in Florida. It appeared like no one could relate to the hunger and thirst that I was experiencing. I spoke to my pastor, and he quickly said I needed to put things in perspective; in other words, get with the program the real deal of living in the United States. I was somewhat disappointed but that did not change my perspective. If anyone knows me from growing up in Jamaica, I was the quietest person on two legs. I would go to school and back and I never got in trouble. For me it was always about the supernatural. I prioritized my relationship with God. More of God was what I desired, however when my new pastor told me to get with the program, I began to do things that I would not normally do. I got caught up with the system, my mindset was shifted, and my hunger for God had diminished. The God I serve is both intentional and purposeful and nothing I tried was working out.

One day the scripture came forcefully to me from *Revelation 3:15,* which states that if I was lukewarm God would spit me out. I was so convicted that I decided to go on a fast. I decided that the duration would be seven days without any food or water. If you ask me today if I knew the proper way to fast, I would tell you "NO" in a heartbeat. I was just passion driven and frustrated with everything that was happening in my life. Fasting was an attempt to get answers from God. I was desperate I had no knowledge of how to fast for such an extensive period. In my ignorance God in His infinite mercies truly covered me. I began fasting and continued after the seven days without food or water. By now hunger was gone from me and all I wanted was more of God. By day fourteen without any food or water my body was becoming weak.

My Mom was doing a live in job, so she had no knowledge of my prolonged fast. My brother was barely home, and my younger sister did not understand much about fasting. I did not share this with anyone because whenever I spoke about the supernatural signs and wonders, miracles, and deliverances they would quickly shut me down. They would mock me and say if I wanted to go up like Elijah. It was now more than fourteen days without food and water. I recall going to church and a fellow parishioner asked me why I looked so weird. My response was, "I am on the Lord's Day," and the response to me was, "every day is the Lord's Day."

The fasting then began to take a toll on my body upon reaching twenty-one days. I could barely do much with my own physical strength, but

God knew I was determined, and I was not about to back down. I was now literally existing on God's grace and mercy each day. My bed was no longer comfortable anymore and so I would throw a blanket and pillow on the floor. The floor was where I would find comfort and peace. Laying on my stomach was the position that brought comfort along with my Bible that was given to me by a very good friend, Raymond Allen, when I was migrating to the United States. To this date it is one of my favorite Bibles even though it is thoroughly marked up, pages pale and discolored and missing pages. I would read it, pray it, and sing it during that fast. It was now day twenty-six and I did not have the strength to go anywhere. I stayed in my room most of the time. My flesh was failing but there was something pushing me; today I call it the hunger and thirst I had for God. I wanted to know Him in a way that was never heard of before. By now you can just imagine, I had lost a lot of weight and the rumors started that I was sick.

One day my pastor called to share that he heard I was sick, he encouraged me to go see a doctor. Respectfully I told him that I was not sick but that I have been fasting for the last twenty – seven days. I remember this so vividly; he was so angry with me. He reprimanded me for doing such nonsense without sharing it with him so he could at least walk me through how to start and end a fast correctly. From that experience I can tell anyone that is desperate for God, make sure it is God and not just a fascination or a mere desire because you can hurt yourself. If it is not a real hunger and thirst after His righteousness, please refrain from going on a fast for thirty days without food and water. No one is advised to do an extensive fast the way I did.

In spite of what my pastor called "nonsense", the good thing about all of this was that my heart was fixed in knowing the supernatural. I was now at a place where it was no longer my flesh but all of God and His glory. God knew my desires and He honored it. At times I felt like giving up as a young Christian because of what I saw. Believers were having a form of godliness but denying the power of God (*2 Timothy 3:5*). When I came to day thirty of my fast without food or water, I received a visitation (supernatural encounter) from the Lord. The clouds were formed in my bedroom and a voice coming from the cloud saying to me, "arise and eat I have heard you and have answered your cry." Now it felt like I was sitting in the clouds and from the right of the room a bright light shone with a staircase leading me to an open room where I saw the sick, lame, dumb, deaf, and even the dead.

The Lord said, "Mary you will be able to do greater works," I opened my mouth and began to sing. I could hear an echo like I had swallowed a sound system. The Lord said from here going forward my voice will be able to project both near and far. To this day that remains a fact. I do not need a microphone to project my voice. God did the unimaginable and I can speak His Word and sing as loud as possible without the aid of a microphone. All of this happened on day thirty of the fast. At this juncture I was reminded that they that hunger and thirst after righteousness shall be filled (*St. Matthew 5:6*). After that encounter and I got back to the natural side of life, and I had strength like never before. My countenance, my speech, and my entire life was changed.

From that day I became fierce in the spirit, I was not afraid of anything that came in my path. This boldness was a result of the encounter I had with the Lord on the thirtieth day of my fast. Well, it took me another thirty days before I regained my taste for food, as I started back with soft foods. However, in the spirit world God had graced me to do things that I would not normally do or even experience. Things were coming from my mouth that even surprised me and lives are now being changed by just being around me. Witnesses would say, "Mary being around you makes me want to change and do the right thing." God reminded me that it was not by might or by power, but it was by His Spirit.

Individuals would often say that there was something about me that challenges them to change. From those thirty days of fasting and prayer my life has never been the same. I can walk in a worship service where the parishioners are not giving God all in worship; however, (without fail) once I open my mouth the atmosphere changes. Even in a funeral service where individuals are mourning the loss of loved ones when I open my mouth to sing, or bring words of comfort, strength and peace would come to the grief stricken through my ministering thus fulfilling the scriptures, *"Blessed are they that mourn for they shall be comforted,"* (*St. Matthew 5:4*)

Despite the challenges at times that come with being graced to be an instrument for His glory, I would not trade this position for all the riches this world can offer. Each time I am faced with a situation where God's divine intervention is needed, I would always ask God to trust me one more time with His grace and that His name be glorified through me.

# CHAPTER TWO – ANTIGUA

## DUTY CALLED AND I ANSWERED AFRAID!

*"Even when I am afraid, I still trust You." – Psalm 56:3*

Antigua and Barbuda are twin-island nation lying between the Caribbean Sea and the Atlantic Ocean. It consists of two major islands, Antigua and Barbuda, and several smaller islands. The islands are low-lying with some higher volcanic areas. Known as the land of 365 beaches, the island is said to have a different beach for every day of the year. Plus, those beaches carry a pinky hue due to the presence of a red shell in the sand grains. This distinctive coloration makes them a sight to behold.

My first call to go to the island of Antigua was when my twin Rachel and Isaiah were three years old. There were so many voices to discourage me, chief of which was that I was crazy leaving my young children behind to do ministry. I felt broken and my spirit was crushed. Feeling overwhelmed and needing guidance I pleaded and called out to the Lord for His help from the depths of my heart. The scripture that came forcefully to my spirit was *St. Mark 10:29 – 31* which states, **"Jesus said, I can guarantee this truth: Anyone who gave up his home, brothers, sisters, mother, father, children, or fields because of me and the Good News 30 will certainly receive a hundred times as much here in this life. They will certainly receive homes, brothers, sisters, mothers, children and fields, along with persecutions. But in the world to come they will receive eternal life. But many who are first will be last, and the last will be first."**

## A prophetic word

*Mark 10:29 - 32* became the anchor in my decision-making process and even though I was broken in my spirit there was yet another pressing hunger and thirst after the manifestation of the Living God. I decided to move forward with the assignment, trusting Him to take care of my children in my absence. My first time in Antigua was for a Women's Retreat and the delegation consisted of seven women including myself. The driver was on time to pick us up at the airport and tried to engage us in a conversation about the island, but to be honest I was more concerned by the distracting noise I heard coming from the back of the van. It sounded like the van was going to break in pieces.

I pointed out the noise I was hearing. He stopped at a mechanic shop to get it looked at. We all disembarked from the van and immediately a well-dressed gentleman came out and approached us. He asked, how we were doing to which we responded that it was good to be on the island. This man of God began to speak directly to me saying, "Woman of God do not worry, the Lord will perfect everything concerning you. All God wants you to do is to continue to be faithful to Him." He continued by assuring me that I have not seen all that God was going to do through me yet. He said my name will not just be called now but for generations to come. He said God wanted me to be concerned about the things that concern Him. He stated that the uncommon favor of God was going to catapult me beyond my wildest dream and that my seams are going to burst open.

I stood in amazement by what I was hearing. I thought I had brought a word to give my sisters in Antigua, but the Lord used His man servant to give me a prophetic word that brought insight, fore sight, and confirmation that the Lord was with me. That was a defining moment and I settled myself in the presence of the Lord and took comfort in knowing that He which hath began a good work in me is well able to complete it (*Philippians 1:6*). Remember our God is wise, and He does all things well. At times He will cause something to go wrong so that destiny and purpose can be fulfilled. The issue with the car resulted in my path to cross with this man of God so I could hear the prophetic word from the Lord.

*Mary L. Daniel-Fuller*

## Woman with unforgiving heart

The first morning of the Women's Retreat I walked in the auditorium for the first service. While praying I saw in the spirit written on the wall, around the four corners of the room the word, "unforgiveness." I then heard the voice of the Lord speak audible to me saying, "my child whatever you say, whatever you do please speak on *St. Luke 1: 1 – 4.* Speak about the fact that there should be no root of bitterness in our hearts." After teaching the Word of God the word of wisdom came alive, and I began to speak as He gave me utterance. I told the ladies someone in our midst is very bitter and God wants to take away that heart of stone and give them a heart of flesh. I stated that no one need to go to hell because God is well able to deliver and bring healing to the heart, one only needed to accept His forgiveness.

A woman began to scream, and she kept on screaming even louder. The Holy Spirit allowed me to identify the place where she was hurting the most. I told her that I understand that the pain is real and that the hurt is great. With the word of knowledge from the Lord, I told her that I knew it cut very deep when her family member threw her out and she did not have anywhere to go. Even though she had a beautiful home and a very good job, she was still so bitter that she could not forgive that family member. Through the inspiration and instruction of the Holy Spirit, I gave her my phone and told her to make that phone call to the family member that had wronged her. In obedience she made the call and the party on the other end answered. She expressed to the individual that she forgave her for the wrong that she did to her. Both parties cried and cried, and immediately I knew that forgiveness had taken place.

## Barren woman conceived and brought forth her child

God continued to manifest Himself during this Women's Retreat. While I was praying the Lord told me that someone came not for themself but for someone else. I stood up and asked aloud, "Who came this weekend not for themself but for another woman?" A woman got up and announced she was the one. I told her what the Lord had instructed me to tell her to do. The person she was representing was married for over nine years and had been trying to have a child. The woman would conceive but by the first trimester she would lose the pregnancy. Through the grace over my life and the instructions by the Holy Ghost I told the woman that was standing in the gap to come forward. I placed my stomach on her stomach and prayed the prayer of faith and told her to go straight to this individual and place her stomach on her and trust God for the miraculous.

Upon my return to Antigua the following year while doing a prayer line, a baby was placed in my hand. The baby was very small, and I knew this baby was special. Someone cried out that this was the baby that the woman stood in the gap for. This was indeed another miracle God once again showed His marvelous works. He is an incredible God who deserves incredible praise, all He wants is for us to be obedient, to what He ask us to do. We do not have to fear or doubt Him, God will do what He says, it has nothing to do with us. All God needs is a vessel that is obedient and dedicated to carry out His work.

## Baby boy named Samuel

One night during the prayer line a pregnant woman came on the line. While praying for her I heard the name Samuel. I told her the name I heard while praying and that this child was going to be a proper child. I also told her she was going to have a safe delivery and that she should call his name Samuel. After the service, the young woman came up to me and she was very upset. She said, "Minister, I know this child is not a boy because I have already given birth to a son and based on the position of the baby, I will be having a girl." She shared all the things that she was experiencing that convinced her that she was carrying a girl. Upon doing the sonogram the gender of the baby was not revealed and the mother was still adamant that this baby was the girl she wanted.

The day of delivery came and my God who never disappoints proved Himself yet again. Sometime after I returned home, the mother called to tell me the baby was a boy as prophesied, and she named him Samuel. All glory and honor belong to God who is the revealer of all secrets. Whenever God speaks, we do not have to second guess what He is saying. That night after I told her what the Lord showed me and she confronted me to disagree with the gender of the child, I did not change what I heard. He still does miracles so great, and He honors His word over His name. *(Psalm 137:2).* When God does something, it is not halfway completed He does it fully to demonstrate that He is in control.

## The healing of my Dad

There are territorial spirits that are assigned to block and to hinder the working of God but rest assured that ALL power belongs to the Almighty God. God can break every chain of darkness and strongholds that causes setbacks. Our God is bigger, stronger, and wiser and He continues to show His mighty hands. My Dad was with me in the Convocation, and he has struggled with back and neck pain most of his life. He had been to several doctors and medication was given but this pain would not go away. On Sunday night, the last night of our Holy Convocation I was not scheduled to preach but my Presiding Bishop earlier in the day had indicated that I would close out the Convocation. While standing in the congregation my Presiding Bishop Lloyd Faulknor introduced me as the preacher of the hour. He mentioned that the hour was set, and we should be open for the Lord to do anything among us.

Once I was given the microphone there was an unprecedented anointing, the Spirit of God was evident in the house. I declared by the Holy Ghost that there will be breakthroughs, deliverance, healing, and restoration. I declared that plenty was about to be released amongst the saints. By now the power of God was not only being displayed but was also being felt. It was like the day of Pentecost. I told the Saints whatever you need to receive it NOW! My Dad was standing directly to my right, and I said to the people through the power of the Holy Ghost, "put your hand wherever you can identify the pain, sickness or disease in your body." I then declared by the power of the Holy Ghost healing in Jesus' name!

My Dad shared with me that by faith he followed the instructions given and touched his back and neck and instantly he felt a fire like sensation penetrating both areas. He was praising God and rejoicing, and I knew it was because the pain that he had endured for years was now gone. Four days later he indicated to me that he was a witness that God was truly a healer. His neck and back pain were gone from that night. I reminded him that the signs would follow those that believe. So many in the service that night received healing and deliverance. Some shared through their testimonies that they have been challenged to walk in their God given abilities. All this is according to one's faith – you also can experience the mighty hand of God. Let Him prove Himself to you. We serve a God that is continuously looking for vessels to be used as an instrument for Him. *2 Timothy 2:21* states that these vessels must be set apart for the Master's use prepared to do every good thing.

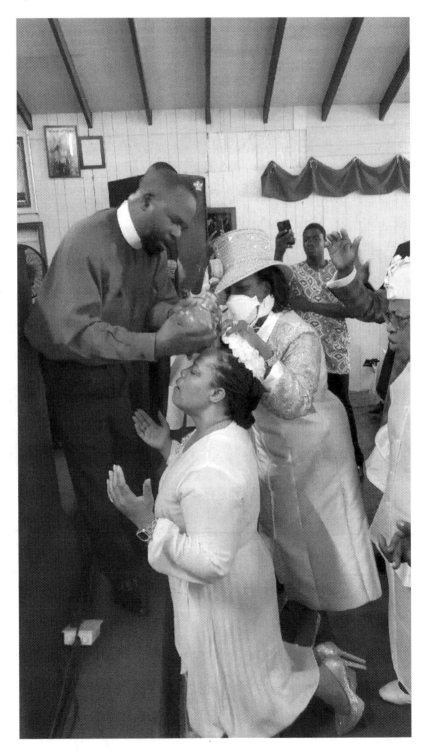

# CHAPTER THREE – CANADA

## THE DISPLAY OF AWESOMENESS

*"O God, your ways are holy! What god is as great as our God? You are the God who performs miracles. You have made your strength known among the nations." - Psalm 77:13-14*

Oh Canada, another country where I experienced divine encounter and miracles signs and wonders being displayed by the Almighty God. We serve a God that we do not have to second guess who He is. Undoubtedly, He does miracles so great. Although I have gone to Canada several times for visitation of loved ones or enjoying a nice vacation, nothing beats being in the presence of God and being used as an instrument for Him. No one can ever deny that when divinity meets humanity your life will never be the same.

### Winnipeg, Manitoba

My first divine encounter happened when visiting a place called Manitoba, Canada which is a Canadian Province bordered by Ontario to the east and Saskatchewan to the west. It is well known for being the home of the polar bear capital of the world. It is the fifth-most populous province, with many beautiful lakes and world class museums along with unique festivals. I remember heading to the airport boarding a flight from John F. Kennedy in New York with a party of five. We were all excited and even though our flights were connecting that did not dampen our spirits, we were going on the Lord's business.

When we got to Winnipeg, Manitoba, I told the team to be very vigilant upon boarding the flight. I was already seated when one of the ladies beckoned to me saying that she wanted to show me something where she was sitting. I was a little irritated because people were still boarding and so it was difficult moving from where I was sitting to where she was. Finally, I got to where she was sitting and what I saw caused me to press the call button and make an alert. There was a big hole where she was sitting it looked like a panel, or something was removed from it. The flight attendant came and then the pilot to looked. Immediately an announcement came was over the PA system that we need to deboard because of mechanical issues. The young woman stated all she could remember was when I told them to be vigilant and stay alert. Her vigilance made her aware of her surroundings and prevented us from flying on a defective aircraft. We had to change planes to continue our trip to Manitoba, Canada. This was one time when a three-hour delay was just fine. We know that miracles do happen every day where God continues to take care of His people and where He allows us to experience grace and mercy.

## Lifted by the Spirit of God

When we got to Manitoba, the immigration officer needed to know why I was visiting Canada, where I was going to be staying and how long I was going to be there. After all that, we got to where we were staying and thanked God for the home that was provided for us. We were all comfortable and I was placed in the visitor's suite that had everything for comfort. I unpacked my luggage and decided to settle down and meditate before my first session of expressing a portion of the Word of God. I laid on the bed on my right side which is my meditative position. As I began to meditate upon the grace of God and the theme that was given for the weekend, I felt like I was being taken up from off the bed. I jumped up and thought to myself maybe it is because I was travelling all morning and having two take offs in such a short space of time it made me feel like I was elevated.

My God will allow you to experience Him in a supernatural way to instill and heighten your faith and trust in Him because of the work that He will do through you. I thought then it was one of two things; I was just having an out of body experience or it was the effect of being jet lagged, from both take offs. I went back to my favorite meditative position and in the Spirit, I was taken up like a baby off the bed and carried to the front door of the house. This was not a dream, or imagination. It was like Philip in *Acts 8:26-40* where he was miraculously transported alongside the Ethiopian eunuch's chariot. The story continues with Philip baptizing the eunuch and the Spirit of the Lord quickly carrying Philip to Azotus where he preached the Gospel in the towns until he reached Caesarea and the eunuch saw him no more.

I have had many spiritual encounters before, but I knew that this one was different. I never experienced being transported in the Spirit like this before. While this was all happening, I heard the voice of God reassuring me that He's with me. Once I was back in my natural state, I called my Pastor who advised me that God is about to do something extra ordinary and that He's about to elevate me to another position. I made another call to one of my mentors who has a way of tapping into the spiritual realm. He walked heavily in the prophetic and he confirmed God's Word. He said that I should trust the process of allowing the power of God to rest upon me, and that I should not be afraid of the unknown. I must submit completely to His will so that the Greater Grace can rest upon me. He also advised me that I need to be sensitive, when I ministered that night, and I must be ready to do exactly what the Holy Ghost would say unto me.

We must be careful who we share our experience with. Although one may say they believe in God, one can also doubt the power of God because of fear or unbelief that God can do great things. *2 Timothy 3:5* states, ***"They will appear to have a godly life, but they will not let its power change them. Stay away from such people."*** It is important that those who you reach out to are aligned with the move and the power of God. I thank God that I could trust the power and move of God on the life of my late pastor and my mentor. The advice they provided me was a great help and a blessing because I was able to follow through with the instructions and it was there that the Lord commanded the blessings. The Bible states, *"without advice plans go wrong, but with many advisers they succeed,"* *(Proverbs 15:22).*

That night when I went to the first service, I knew God had prepared me for something I had never seen before. We were in an inter-tribal culture of Native Americans. For my team and I it was a different culture, territorial spirits, different beliefs, spiritual rituals, different ways of worship etc. Right there I understood that God made no mistakes in allowing me to experience the next level of the supernatural because of the rituals and customs that I would encounter in this territory. Now the gift of the Word of knowledge was activated, and the Lord gave me the first scripture. He told me that I should tell the people according to *1 Corinthians 2:1-5* *"Brothers and sisters when I came to you, I didn't speak about God's mystery as if it were some kind of brilliant message or wisdom, while I was with you, I decided to deal with only one subject – Jesus Christ, who was crucified when I came to you, I was weak. I was afraid and very nervous. I didn't speak my message with persuasive intellectual arguments. I spoke my message with a show of spiritual power, so that your faith would not be based on human wisdom but on God's Power."*

Once I echoed these verses, the Holy Ghost began to move mightily in the congregation. There was a disturbance to try and kill that which God hath purposed to do such as spiritual wickedness and spirits that come against the Spirit of the Living God. I could hear clearly in the Spirit realm that I should take authority over every area of the building. I began to declare in the atmosphere, "He shall give His angels charge over me and to keep me in all my ways. We wrestle not against flesh blood, but against principalities, against the rulers of darkness, and against spiritual wickedness in high places," *(Psalm 91:11; Ephesians 6:12).* I called upon the God that answers by fire, just like he did for Elijah on Mount Carmel when he was up against the prophets of Baal, He answered my prayers, *(1 Kings 18: 24 – 40).*

*Lady with pins and screws in her right hand*

The Greater Grace, the Greater Power and the God of all God's began to demonstrate Himself. That night the Holy Ghost directed me to a lady, and I told her that she was in a bad car accident and her right hand was severely damaged. The Spirit of the Lord showed me that she had pins and hooks in her right hand, she had struggled when she should come to the service.

I told her by faith to lift her right hand and watch God do a miracle. She said she could not because of the pins in her hand. Through the power of the Holy Ghost, I took her by the right hand and lifted it up over her head. She began to scream saying "Thank you Jesus, Hallelujah, Lord, I thank you for doing what I could not do for over a year." Just like that it happened. The severity of the injury prevented her from putting her hand over her head but now through the power of God, she was praising God. The people who knew her recognized that that they had just witnessed a miracle. Their hearts were now open because of the manifestations and prophesies that were unveiling before their faces. This caused them to tap in and allow the Holy Ghost to have His way. Many were delivered and set free as they exercised their faith in the Lord.

## Salvation to the whole family

While being led by the Spirit, I called for all the youth that were in the congregation. I had never seen so many young people in one circle for a local service. There was a little lad not more than twelve years old. When he came up to me, I could tell from the look on his face he was desperate for God. When he was next in line he was trembling and shaking under the divine presence of the Lord. I asked him, "What do you want the Lord to do for you?" He put both hands around me, his head in my chest, cried on top of his lungs and said: "Save my mother, save my grandmother, Lord Jesus, just save my family!" He spoke with such fervency that my bowels of compassion were released.

The Holy Ghost directed me to ask where the mother of the young lad was. From the back of the sanctuary there came a young woman weeping. I recognized that she needed salvation. She cried and cried,

I told her under the power of the Holy Ghost that because of the cry of her son, salvation has come to her house. Immediately, the power of God fell, and she was filled with the Holy Ghost with the evidence of speaking in tongues. God once again showed up, so many generational curses, customs, spirit of depression, and oppression were broken. Our God goes beyond cultures, nation, color, class, or creed to save us. *St. John 3:16* states, ***"God loved the world this way: He gave his only Son so that everyone who believes in him will not die but will have eternal life."*** These signs will continue to be fulfilled for them that believe.

## *Woman that wanted the anointing I have*

While in the service I called for a prayer line for those who needed something specific from God. A woman came in the prayer line, and I asked her what she wanted from God. She stated the same anointing and grace that I had upon my life. Through the leading of the Holy Ghost, I told her to stand to my right as I continued to pray for others on the line. After I was finished with those on the line, I went over to her and asked her if she was fasting and praying for this kind of anointing. Her response was she fast occasionally. I told her that to get this level of anointing she had to be consistent with her prayer life and her hunger must measure up to what she desired.

The Holy Ghost then directed me to lay hands upon her and immediately she fell to the floor. She remained there as the Lord continue to deal with her. The Bible states in *2 Timothy 2: 20 -22*, ***"In a large house there are not only objects made of gold and silver, but also those made of wood and clay. Some objects are honored when they are used; others aren't. Those who stop associating with dishonorable people will be honored. They will be set apart for the master's use, prepared to do good things."***

As the Lord continued to move in the service lives were being transformed as many individuals began to publicly rededicate their lives to the Lord. Others were challenged to walk in their purpose and their giftings. The outpouring of the Holy Ghost was rich in the house as those present basked in His presence. During all this the lady was still on the floor as the Lord was dealing with her, she could not contain the power and the grace of God that was now upon her life. She had to be carried out of the sanctuary when the service was dismissed.

## The province of Ontario

The province of Ontario is another beautiful place where God again has no respect of location or persons. Toronto is the capital city, and it is the most populous city in Canada and the fourth most populous city in North America. Toronto is ranked as one of the most multicultural metropolises in the world with half of its population born outside Canada. I know that God who is bigger than provinces, cities, towns, and cultures always has His people in mind. I was invited to minister the Word of God in a Men's and Women's conference. One of the sisters who had accompanied me twisted her ankle which immediately began to swell, and she could not put any pressure on it. We went to the house where we were staying, and individuals were saying she should go to the hospital because of the severity of the injury and that it will only get worse.

I was not worried I said to everyone softly being led by the Holy Ghost, "Let God be God." We circled her, anointed her foot with oil, and I prayed the prayer of faith. The next morning when she got up miraculously by the power of God her foot was healed. God did it again! She skipped, jumped, danced, and gave praises unto the Almighty God. There's nothing impossible for our God to do, His Word declares, **"What you have believed will be done for you!"** St. Matthew 9:29. During those services people were baptized in Jesus' name and were also filled with the Holy Ghost. We are encouraged to walk by faith and not by sight because this supernatural power requires faith. The Bible declares, **"So, faith comes from hearing the message, and the message that is heard is what Christ spoke,"** (Romans 10:17).

Let us understand that power belongs to God and we all can be conduit of this same power. God is still looking for individuals that are submissive, obedient, and disciplined enough to carry out His orders.

The supernatural power of God can only be experienced when the difficult situation becomes impossible and where God Himself shows up and shows to us that it is not by might nor by power but by the Spirit. Whenever you get a taste of the power of God, you will never be the same because the power of God is transformative. Are you available to be used by Him? Do you want to experience the supernatural power of God? The Word of God declares: *"Whoever comes to me will never go hungry and whoever believes in me will never be thirsty,"* *(St. John 6:35)*. It is through our hunger that God fulfills our desires, *St. Matthew 5:6* states, *"Blessed are those who hunger and thirst for God's approval. They will be satisfied."*

## Young girl received the gift of the Holy Ghost with power

As I was ministering the Sunday morning of the Men and Women's Conference that I was attending a young girl came up to me and stated that she wanted the anointing I had on my life. I instructed her to wrap her arms around me as I embraced her and placed my stomach on hers. Immediately as I did that there was a transfer of power. She leaped up in the air and was speaking in other tongues as the Spirit of God gave her utterance. God honored her request by filling her with the Holy Ghost instantly. God promises that if we seek Him, we will find Him. He encourages us to ask, and it shall be given unto us according to the plan and purpose for our lives.

## Woman with walking stick healed

In that same service a woman came in using a walking stick. She came up for prayer and I took the consecrated oil and anointed her knee. I uttered the words, be healed in Jesus' name," and the woman immediately threw away the walking stick and started running around the sanctuary praising God. The saints began to rejoice as they beheld the miracle and the demonstration of the power of God. God reminded me that it was according to our faith.

At times we do not derive the blessings and the miracles that God has for us because we fail to exercise our faith and trust in Him. In *St. Matthew 13:58*, it states that Jesus did not do many miracles in His own country, NOT because He could not, but because of the lack of faith of those present. We MUST exercise our faith to get the results we need from God. If one does not have strong desires for the presence of God and to know more of Him, then most likely one will receive based on their desire. May you find the courage to step out of your comfort zone so that God can be glorified in you. Remember that the path to experiencing more of God, is deeply personal and the price for divine encounters is death to self.

# CHAPTER FOUR – ISRAEL

## A DREAM BECAME REALITY

*"Be happy with the Lord and He will give you the desires of your heart.*
*Entrust your ways to the Lord, trust Him and He will act on your behalf."*
*Psalm 37:4-5*

As a child growing up there were some places that I thought to myself was not on earth and one of them was Israel. So, to even get to a place where I could experience the different places where Jesus Christ the Messiah walked was amazing. Seeing places like the streets of Jerusalem and the Sea of Galilee were life changing experiences. Come with me as I share the divine encounter with the Lord. I remember so clearly when the opportunity presented itself for me to go to the Holy Land, I was so excited and thrilled. I was told to bring comfortable shoes, enough sun block and most of all come with an open heart to receive that which the Lord had in store.

What I am about to share are very special moments recorded during my visit. My very good friend Pastor David Linton was on this trip. We have shared several mission trips together but this one was exceptional for both of us. Like Jonathan and David, our friendship was not just brothers and sisters, but we shared a similar hunger and thirst to know the supernatural power of the Almighty God. As we sailed together on the Sea of Galilee, I received much education. All along before this visit I thought this was a sea but rather it was a big lake. Our tour guide educated us that even though it was called the Sea of Galilee by tradition, it was the lowest freshwater lake on earth and the second lowest lake in the world after the Dead Sea.

## Wailing Wall

Each day we would visit different historical places. I remember one of our stops was the Western Wall (Hebron Ha – Kotel – Ha Ma aravi); also called the Wailing Wall in the Old City of Jerusalem. It is a place of prayer and pilgrimage sacred to the Jewish descendants. This is the place where the Jews gathered to express gratitude to God or pray for divine mercy. Our tour guide explained that after the temple was destroyed in 70 AD, the Jews were exiled from the city, and it became a place of pilgrimage where they would lament their loss.

There is also a section of the wall dedicated for a source of comfort and consolation for the misfortune. When I got to the Wailing Wall, what an amazing sight to see people of all walks of life. I had asked my loved ones to give me their prayer requests before I left home so that when I got there, I could put it in between the opening of the rocks. My God, my Savior when I drew closer to the wall, I could feel the divine presence of the Almighty God. When I touched the wall itself, I felt something that I never experienced. There was a young Jewish lady next to me and I knew she was not just a Jew but a Christian Jew. With tears running down her face, I could relate as I felt the tears flowing from my eyes. I knew there was something powerful emanating from this Wall. On one hand I was on earth touching an ancient wall, while at the same time my spiritual eyes were opened and I saw clouds, on which angels and seraphim descended and ascended.

I was taken up in the spirit where I saw a seraph, who brought to me a key and I heard a voice out of the cloud saying, "I am with you always, do not let your pain and disappointment cripple you. What you are experiencing is only to perfect that which concerns you." The key from the seraph was an indication that doors would be locked and unlocked for His purposes throughout my life. When I came back to myself, I realized that this was not a dream but rather another divine encounter. That day put everything in perspective for me, that God is with me and that all things were for my good. This was the beginning of the greater grace being displayed during the rest of my trip in Israel.

## Mount Carmel

Getting to the place called Mount Carmel where Elijah proved again that our God is Almighty. Altars were built up and soaked with water, yet the power of the Living God came down and showed Himself strong *(1 Kings 18)*. Another place that came alive was the River Jordan where Jesus Himself was baptized and the voice from heaven echoed, ***"This is my beloved son in whom I am well pleased,"*** *(St. Matthew 3: 13 - 17)*. I had the opportunity to minister to two ladies, a mother, and daughter. They were curious why I had this smile that would light up any room I occupied. I told her it was because the love of God was in my heart. I further shared that I was baptized in Jesus' name and believed in the infilling of the Holy Ghost which gives me joy, and that joy is unstoppable.

## Baptism of seven souls in River Jordan

After sharing my testimony, the mother asked me, when I get to River Jordan if I can baptize her in the name of Jesus Christ. She stated that she wanted to experience the same joy. I told her that my friend Pastor Linton would assist me with the baptism. Instead of only baptizing that one individual we baptized seven souls. It appeared that everything stood still as we were doing the baptism, the people around were amazed at how we were doing the baptism. We were baptizing them in the name of the Lord Jesus Christ for the remission of their sins. I wanted to be baptized in the River Jordan not for salvation, but symbolically because Jesus Christ Himself was baptized there; however, if you eat meat and it offends your brother do not eat meat. I did not get baptized because there were those in the delegation who felt that baptism should only be done once. But our God is *tricky-fi,* for I did not get baptized, but I had the opportunity to baptize seven souls. *★Tricky-fi – God's way of turning a situation inside out and upside down to make it work.*

## The Dead Sea

The Dead Sea was another place that intrigued me. Our tour guide gave us the relevant scriptures of the Dead Sea so that the scriptures would come alive as we walked and experienced it. The Dead Sea was also called the Salt of Lake bordered by Jordan to the East and West bank, and Israel to the west. It has the lowest elevation and the lowest body of water on earth. Along with being incredibly salty, no macroscopic aquatic organisms such as fish or water plants can live in it, however it contains microbial life. According to *Colossians 1:16-17*, **"He created all things in heaven visible and invisible, whether they are kings or lords or powers, everything has been created through Him and for Him. He existed before everything and held everything together."**

What a mighty God we serve! I encountered again the healing power of God through going into the Dead Sea. I used crystal salt and minerals to rub all over my body and my face that had pimples and blotches of discoloration. Immediately, I felt a burning sensation over my skin as I began touching my skin it was very smooth to the touch and there were no pimples. Upon returning to my hotel room and after taking my shower my skin still felt like that of a newborn baby; very soft to the touch and the pimples had all miraculously disappeared. All praise belongs to our God!

## Old city of Jerusalem

My last encounter while visiting Israel was when we were going overnight to stay in the Old City of Jerusalem. Once again, our tour guide provided us all the relevant scriptures that whenever we got to the city everything would make sense as the Biblical account would come alive. Now again I thought Jerusalem was in heaven and not on earth. Upon arriving in Old Jerusalem, the driver of the bus began to play a well-known hymn, "Jerusalem, Jerusalem, lift up your gates and sing; hosanna in the highest, hosanna to your King." The driver then told everyone over the intercom to turn our heads to the left, to look over into the city of Jerusalem. As I turned and looked the sight was too much to behold. No man can see God and live, so what God did once again for me was to show me a glimpse of His sovereignty. This time I saw angelic beings flapping their wings. I thought to myself I was just tired, and I was seeing things, however when the bus stopped, and we began to look over the city I stood in awe of God's majestic glory; what I saw was real.

I heard a voice spoke these words, "I am the Lord thy God, I will show you signs and wonders in days and years to come." My feet became weak, and I could hardly stand. Upon reaching the hotel I got my luggage and was given the key to my room. I swiftly went to my room where the Lord appeared as a bright light; the light shone like it was the mid-day sun. I was amazed as I saw an angelic being with wings opened that filled the room. This was like *Isaiah 6:1-2* where the scripture states that, **"I saw the Lord sitting on a high and lofty throne. The bottom of His robe filled the temple. Above Him stood the seraphim; each had six wings with two (each) covered his own face."**

I spent the night on my belly and my face experiencing the glory of the Lord. That night, God worked on my heart because it was bitter. He worked on my mind because I was thinking of doing things that would have never brought Him glory. I had just gone through a divorce and the shame, and the abuse was eating me out like cancer, but God showed up once again and gave me a brand-new heart and a right spirit. After that encounter, especially being in the Holy Land, confirmed once again that every word spoken by my mother was coming to pass indeed. I was a special child. In every part of my trip to Israel my eyes were opened to the great mystery of God. What an experience walking the grounds of a place called Masada. It is an ancient fortress located in the Southern Israel's Judean Dessert, a mountain where you can overlook the Dead Sea.

There is a portion that is highlighted among the ruins of King Herod's Palace that sprawls over three rock terraces. It is the last stand of Jewish patriots in the face of the Roman army in 73 AD. It was built as a palace complex in the classic style of the early Roman Empire by Herod the Great King of Judea (Reigned 37- 4 BC). I learned that in the Hebrew, the meaning of Masada is strong foundation or support. We got to the top of the mountain by cable cars.

Even though it was scary, it was a great experience. To tell you everything that happened it would not be possible in this book. While walking in the Roman Colosseum built by Herod, the largest amphitheater in the ancient world, I had the opportunity to form a quick singing group. We sang a few songs, and we did not need a microphone because this place had the natural air that amplified our voices. More highlights include walking in the coarse sand of the Mediterranean Sea, swimming in the Sea of Galilee, being in the Garden of Gethsemane, taking the Lord's Supper in the area near Golgotha and experiencing a replica of a tomb used by Jesus was magnificent and will be forever etched in my memory. I also purchased the anointed prayer shawl that I currently use as a point of contact whenever the Lord directs me to do so. My prayer shawl is very dear to me. I use it like the Apostle Paul's handkerchiefs and aprons that was used for healing and driving out evil spirits *(Acts 19:1)*. Whenever I am going somewhere for the first time to minister, I bring my prayer shawl with me as a tangible reassurance that God is with me.

*Mary L. Daniel-Fuller*

# CHAPTER FIVE – JAMAICA

## SIGNS AND WONDERS WILL FOLLOW
## THEM THAT BELIEVE

*"Show Your power by healing and performing miracles and doing amazing things in the power of your Holy servant Jesus Christ." – Acts 4:30*

It is said that Jamaica is the largest island of the commonwealth in the Caribbean and the third largest of the Greater Antilles. Even though Jamaica is famous for its beaches, food, and music it is recorded to have the most churches per square kilometers than anywhere else in the world. However, mingled amongst all these churches are evidence of the works of the devil but the miraculous power of God is still being manifested in the fourteen parishes.

### Anointed to sing

My first encounter of these signs on the island was when I was only fourteen years old and a young believer of the faith. Being fascinated and passionate about the work of the Holy Ghost, wherever my pastor, the late Bishop B.S.E. Dyer would go I would be there. I was not deterred by the glaring knowledge that I had school the next day. I had a deep hunger and thirst for the manifestation and demonstration of the Holy Ghost in me and around me.

One day, my church Rehoboth was having a crusade in Top Hill, Clarendon.

Our church bus left from Lot 1 Augusta Drive, Independence City, St. Catherine headed by our late Bishop Dyer who was telling us something wonderful was going to happen. He kept saying something supernatural is going to happen. Upon arriving in the district, there was a big white tent, no chairs were inside, plywood boards laid across two blocks and those were our seats. No one was there from the community, the attendees consisted of only those of us who had travelled on the bus and our pastor's car.

Service began and when it came to offering time my Bishop stated, "I am going to ask Junior Missionary Mary Daniel to sing while the offering is being collected." I was very astonished because I could barely hold a note to save my life and I did not consider myself a singer. Notwithstanding, I stood up in obedience to my Pastor's request even though I was shaking. My cousins who were the singing birds started to mockingly say, "Is Bishop out of his mind?" Ignoring their comments, I continued to make my way to the front of the tent and took the microphone. I closed my eyes and started to sing a well-known song, "Why don't you turn, turn around; why do you roam, don't you see the Father is waiting to welcome you home." As I was singing, I saw a cloud shaped like a man's right hand with the index finger pointing at me and with a loud voice that echoed said, "Open your mouth." I did as I was commanded, and the index finger of the cloud touched my tongue and from that day, everything about my voice was changed. The finger that touched my tongue changed my voice from being a sound in the crowd to being one that attracts the hearer and points them towards the Savior.

When I opened my eyes, the tent was now filled with people from the community crying out to the Lord and surrendering their lives to Jesus Christ. It became very clear that I was an instrument graced to be used by Him. I was amazed that the Lord used my voice to usher the residents of the community to come into the tent. That night souls were saved, and God got the glory. I went home feeling especially blessed that God chose to use me.

### Divine protection

Walking home late at night after church services in areas where hard crimes took place, I had no fear. I was a young girl, with no transportation to get me to and from services; therefore, my only option was to walk. I believed that God had the power to shield and safeguard me from harm and danger. I trusted God's protection to bring comfort and peace of mind as I walked home nightly. I knew I had His protection because those were dangerous streets where women were being raped, individuals were shot, robbed and some being killed. In all this God shielded me from the hands of the violent men. On the way home I would recite Psalm 91 that assured me that I do not need to fear terrors of the night, arrows that fly during the day, and the plagues that roam the dark.

## Healed from white puss filled pimples all over my body

My next encounter of the supernatural happened, when my Mom migrated to Canada, leaving my siblings and I on the island with my eldest sister Carol. This was a very challenging period in my life because she had no interest in me going to church. She would manufacture all kinds of excuses for me not to go to church. It went from babysitting my niece to saying it was too late for me to be on the road at nights. Nevertheless, I purposed in my heart to always seek and chase after God while making Him my priority.

One day while taking my shower I noticed white-like puss coming from all over my body. I was scared out of my wits and did not know how to tell my sister. I mustered the courage to share it with one of my cousins who was so concerned and afraid for me. This went on for fourteen days and my concern was now heightened. One evening after taking my shower the white puss began to ooze over my body as usual. I knelt right there in the bathroom and prayed this prayer of faith, "Lord if you heal me from this sickness or whatever disease this is that is plaguing my body, I will serve you for the rest of my life." Immediately, I felt fire permeating from the top of my head to my toes. Instantly I knew that I had gotten healing from the Lord. I showered the next day and told my cousin to come and look. The fire of God burned out every sickness that was in my body – no more white puss. Lord let your name be glorified!

## Demon possessed woman

I remember so clearly while being called to an assignment in Kingston with a well-known organization that the Holy Ghost was evident in the house. A young lady came up for prayer. Through the inspiration of the Holy Ghost, I recognized that she was bound with unclean spirits that could not tolerate the divine presence of God. She began to disturb the move of God. Through the grace of God over my life, I began to assure the people of God that it was not by might nor by power, but it was by the Spirit of the Living God. I commanded the unclean spirit by the Holy Ghost to leave her body. The unclean spirit responded and said, "I am not going anywhere." I asked the spirit, "Who sent you?" the unclean spirit responded, "Paula."

This situation was like the man in *St. Mark 5: 5 – 17* that was possessed with demons and stated that his name was Legion. I took authority by the greater power, which is the Holy Ghost and told those around me with unbelief, fear, and doubts to step aside. I submitted myself to be used as an instrument for Him. I asked for a bottle of water, consecrated it through prayer, and told the young lady to drink it. She followed the instruction and with no exaggeration in two gulps she began to vomit things that could not be identified with the natural eyes, but through the Spirit one could tell that this woman was delivered from the demon that possessed her. Black, green, and even red slimy and frothy things were coming up.

I then told her to call Jesus three times and when she began to call on the name of Jesus something supernatural happened. Again, the Holy Ghost fell upon everyone in the house and the young woman that was just delivered received the gift of the Holy Ghost with the evidence of speaking in tongues. No one had to tell her she was delivered and filled. After everything was done, I had seated her in a seat on the rostrum. When one of the ushers was trying to get her to change seats, she said,

"Mi good now, the Pastor placed me fe siddung and mi good!" (I am good now, the pastor placed me to sit, and I am good.) Whom the Son set free is free indeed. What a night it was in the house of the Lord! All praises belong to the Almighty God; these signs shall follow them that believe was fulfilled in the house that night. Signs are not only for the unbelievers but also for anyone who desire to experience the supernatural. If you desire a deeper encounter with God, ask and it shall be given; seek and you shall find. God promised that He will give thee the desires of thine heart.

## A mighty outpouring - 21 received the gift of the Holy Ghost

The outpouring of the Holy Ghost was first recorded in the book of Acts. On the day of Pentecost according to *Acts 1:1- 4*, the disciples were with one accord and the Holy Ghost fell upon them and they began to speak as the Spirit gave them utterance. I have often sung the song, "Pentecost can be repeated for the Lord is just the same." That night I had that encounter.

It was another beautiful day as I was getting ready to minister the Word, there was an intangible presence of the Lord in the room. I knew from previous exposure to the presence of God, on that level that something supernatural was going to happen. It was in the parish of St. Elizabeth at a Holy Convocation where individuals from the island and overseas were present. As I was introduced to the congregation and stepped in the pulpit, it felt like lightening and thunderbolts in the sanctuary. It was like electricity distributed evenly. The presence of the Lord was clearly evident. The Holy Ghost fell upon us. I have never seen or heard in my circle at one given time twenty-one received the gift of the Holy Ghost and spoke with other tongues as the Spirit gave them utterance.

## A mighty outpouring - 19 received the gift of the Holy Ghost

God needed me to know that He was the one that does all things great and mighty. The following evening, I was scheduled again to deliver the Word and while His people were worshipping; this time the Holy Ghost came like a mighty wind and nineteen persons received the gift of the Holy Ghost. Seven souls were baptized in the name of Jesus Christ. I was so blessed and encouraged to see the move of God and with tears in my eyes, I gave God thanks that out of all the people He had to choose, He chose me.

## Woman healed who could not walk

In the same service where the nineteen souls received the gift of the Holy Ghost, there was a woman that was sick and could not walk; she had a stick to aid her. When the Holy Ghost fell in the room, miraculously she stood up, walking, leaping, and rejoicing in the God of our salvation. He is the God of all flesh and there is nothing that is too hard for Him to do. Believers' faith was strengthened by the tangible evidence of this miracle. The Holy Ghost was everywhere that night and individuals who were possessed with demons were also delivered.

## Woman with breast cancer healed

That same night the Holy Ghost took me over to a young woman that was struggling with breast cancer. As I walked up to her, I told her that the Great Physician was in the house and that the grace of God over my life had directed me to her. I also told her the specific breast that was affected, as I held her hand, I told her that God wanted to heal her. I placed my right hand directly on the breast with the cancer. I prayed the prayer of faith and suddenly there was fire coming from my hand. As I felt it, I knew instantly that God was doing a miraculous work upon this woman. She began to scream saying, "Jesus, Jesus, thank you Jesus!"

I do not make it a habit to give out my telephone number to individuals when I go on assignment. However, I was prompted by the Holy Ghost to give her my number. Two weeks later I got a call from a number I did not recognize. With great exclamation and rejoicing the person at the other end of the line indicated that she was the woman with the cancer in her breast that I prayed for. She shared that she had gone to the doctor and the good news was there was no sign of cancer and no scar tissues, no sign that this "BIG C" was ever in her breast. I began to share in her rejoicing and thanksgiving, once again God had proven Himself to be the Balm in Gilead.

Our God is purposeful and deliberate, that when He does anything He removes all trace of affliction. This is done so that we can understand that He is God, and He doeth all things well! Being used by God is not confined to pastors, preachers, teachers, bishops, apostles, or those with titles. This can happen to anyone when we avail ourselves to the Almighty and become flexible in His hands. As the Lord started using me in this capacity, I began to doubt myself, thinking that these great signs and wonders can only be done through individuals with titles. I felt like an imposter unworthy of the grace that was now so evident over my life. How mistaken I was, to this date God continues to use me as His instrument.

The Holy Ghost reminded of the scripture found in *2 Timothy 2:20-21*, ***"In a large house there are not only objects made of gold and silver, but also those made of wood and clay. Some objects are honored when they are used; others aren't. Those who stop associating with dishonorable people will be honored. They will be set apart for the master's use, prepared to do good things."*** From that day, the revelation of the scripture served as fuel for me to seek God in a new way. I set aside time for fasting where God revealed to me that I should fast the first seven days of each month. He instructed me that it should be a time of prayer and consecrating of myself so that the power of God can continue to rest upon me. Initially this seemed like a lot, but I quickly embraced the instruction knowing that if I wanted MORE, I had to do MORE!

It is important to note that signs and wonders are designed by God. They are both used to describe extraordinary events that indicate the presence or action of God. I believe God not only for healing but for the saving of souls, for the infilling of the Holy Ghost, and deliverance from the powers of darkness. I have experienced God on different breath, length, forms and shapes and I want to remind you that our God is the same yesterday, today and forever. In *St. John 14:12* it states, **"I can guarantee this truth: Those who believe in me will do the things that I am doing. They will do even greater things because I am going to the Father."** And so, my hunger for His presence got stronger. My desire came with sleepless nights, and my appetite could not be satisfied with only the healing of a headache. I needed to see the signs and wonders of God in a greater grace.

At times I would be mocked and jeered because of my discipline and the sacrifice I made. I was seeking God for the manifestation of the supernatural, it was not so that I could be seen or heard or acquire a personal stage or have my name in bright lights. This was solely so that God could be glorified! If He was going to use anyone, I wanted to be THAT vessel. Consecrated and useful for the Master. I was strengthened by the story of Elijah and Elisha *(2 Kings 2)*. Elisha was mocked and told, **"Do you know that the Lord is going to take your master from you today?"**. Elisha kept on following Elijah wherever he went. Elisha endured being laughed at, mocked, and was even called names but he kept following because he had a desire that needed to be filled. He wanted a double portion of Elijah's spirit to be upon him. The Word of God served as encouragement for me to keep pressing until God was fully formed in me.

These miracles, signs, and wonders are just a few that stood out to me while ministering in the island of my birth – Jamaica! My highest honor and the greatest desire that I have is for God to continue to trust me with His grace. I want to continue to serve as a channel through which He can function to bring healing and deliverance to His people.

# CHAPTER SIX – NEPAL

## THE GOD OF ALL GODS!

*"In this way all the people of the world will know that the L*ORD *is God and there is no other god." - 1 King 8:60*

When I first heard about Nepal never did it cross my mind that I would have an opportunity to minister there. A Missionary of my assembly had gone there before and so when the opportunity was given to me, I did not hesitate. I took it as another advantage to spread the gospel of Jesus Christ, and to reach the lost at any cost. Nepal is a landlocked country in South Asia and is bordered by China and India. It is in the Himalayas and contains eight of the world's ten highest peaks. Nepal is a secular country with Hinduism and Buddhism as the major religions. Hinduism is practiced by roughly 81% of the population and Buddhism by approximately 9%.

One of the most profound attributes of God is his omnipresence - the fact that He is always present everywhere. The Bible clearly teaches that there is no place where God's presence does not extend. This has important implications for how we understand God and how we live our lives. While the main religion is not Christianity, God sure has a way of manifesting His presence. Because God is everywhere, we can never be outside of His sight or knowledge. *Hebrews 4:13* says, **"No creature can hide from God. Everything is uncovered and exposed for Him to see. We must answer to Him."**

## Divine protection while travelling

It took us two days of traveling to get to the place where service would be held. The flight from John F. Kennedy airport to Dubai took approximately fourteen hours and then another flight from Dubai to Katmandu, Nepal was another six hours. Katmandu is the capital, so we had to travel by a van for another eight hours to get to a place called Rauthat. It has one of the highest percentages of Muslim people. Their main language is Nepali, and their second spoken language is Maithili. We were among regions and territories that did not embrace the supernatural power of the Holy Ghost, however, the scriptures that kept me going on this mission trip were *Ephesians 6:12,* **"This is not a wrestling match against a human opponent. We are wrestling with rulers, authorities, the powers who govern this world of darkness, and spiritual forces that control evil in the heavenly world."** And *Psalm 91:11,* **"He will put his angels in charge of you to protect you in all your ways."**

Upon arrival we were met by the local pastor, who was also passionate about the sovereignty of God. He gave us his testimony of becoming a Christian and the ministry work that he has been doing on that side of the vineyard. The first thing that stood out to me was their culture and lifestyle. I had a light bulb moment when individuals shared what they had to go through just to be saved or to experience the power of God. As I listened and processed the information, I was receiving I thought to myself that my two days of traveling was nothing in comparison to what these saints had to go through. Instead, I gave God thanks for the provision that He made for me to be there to share His Word.

One of the stories that stood out to me was the journey that some had taken to get to the service. They had to walk through rivers, being wet, having their bags over their heads making sure that their Bible did not get wet. Walking from mountains, dirt roads, and some for one day others for two days. They were determined and desperate to experience God in a special way. When I heard, my body shook and my spirit man was so overwhelmed to hear such stories. I began to talk with the individuals that came with me on this trip. I told them to seize this opportunity and make sure that when we leave, we should leave a portion of God's grace, power, and His will to everyone that will be here during these days.

Because of the language differences I needed an interpreter, and so a couple of God's people were assigned to us including the pastor that picked us up from the airport. It was my first time being in a service where I needed an interpreter. My first session was a little challenging, however I knew from the Holy Ghost that the Word of God was being received and that I could not look from a man's perspective but through the lens of the Spirit of God. It was a three-day conference and we had hundreds of women not including men and children hungry for the presence of God, they wanted more. During my next session once I took the microphone, I began to worship God, and my interpreter and dear sister was also in-tune with the Holy Ghost. Whatever the Holy Ghost commanded me to say, I said, and she told them. I did not alter or change anything because this is directly from the Lord irrespective of their culture.

We worshipped for half an hour, and the atmosphere was ready for the gift of prophesy to operate, where healing can be experienced and where lives can be transformed for His glory. The Spirit of God revealed to me that some of the women had tumors, and some had bacteria because of improper hygiene practice. God is faithful to His Word, I remembered the scripture taken from *St. Matthew 10: 7-8*, **"As you go, spread this message. The kingdom of heaven is near, cure the sick, bring the dead back to life, cleanse those with skin diseases and force demons out people. Give these things without charging since you received them without paying."**

## Women healed from various sicknesses and delivered from demons

I began to administer what God said to do, I asked for bottles of water and told them that they needed to drink because healing waters are flowing. All those who drank from those bottles of water in that session experienced the healing power of God. Some of the ladies were vomiting stuff that could not be identified with the natural eyes. In the spirit realm I knew it was uncleanness. That night individuals were being healed from various sicknesses and delivered from demons. There were no dry eyes in that session, tears of joy, tears of hope, tears of faith and confidence in God saying, I am next in line for a miracle.

## Graced to speak Nepali as the Spirit gave me utterance

On the last day of the conference, I thought to myself after such a great encounter of so many lives being healed and delivered what more could be done. The God that we serve, His ways and thoughts are higher than our ways, and He is always up to something that we can never imagine. On that morning there was only one session for the day because everyone had to return home, and their journey would be long. Praise and worship was in full action and the Holy Ghost was in operation; the saints were giving thanks for all the things that He had done that morning. They called this Holy Ghost Rally. The ladies were there standing with their hands held high crying out to the Lord, and I gave the relevant instructions on how to receive the gift of the Holy Ghost through the help of the interpreter.

As I was speaking the Holy Ghost began to move, and something miraculous happened. I began to speak in a language that I never spoke before, the interpreter looked at me with great amazement. I did not know what was happening but one thing I knew, was that it was something marvelous. The same thing I was saying the interpreter was saying. The Lord allowed me in that moment to speak in their language. I have never spoken in another language under the power of the Holy Ghost before, all power and glory belong to the Almighty God. I cannot claim Nepali as a language that I speak because that was not my doing, and it was only for that moment. So many received the gift of the Holy Ghost with the evidence of speaking in tongues as the Holy Ghost gave them utterance.

The roads in Nepal are not the safest, I remember on the day while travelling by car the clouds were thick. I was concerned about the driver's ability to see with such thick fog and made mention of my concern to one of the pastors that was on the trip. He said, "Pastor Mary," and I looked into his face and knew that it was only God that was guiding us along this treacherous journey. When you looked down on both sides of the road there was nothing. If the vehicle went over, you would not even be found. I began to pray; "Lord, I know you did not bring me here to leave me. Do what no one else can do, bring us safety, bring protection to this vehicle even now." I then repeated the latter part of *Psalms 23*, ***"Even though I walk through the dark valley of death, because you are with me, I fear no harm, your rod and your staff give me courage."*** *Psalms 91:10-11* also served to provide me with comfort and confidence, ***"No harm will come to you; He will put his angels in charge of you to protect you in all your ways. They will carry you in their hands."*** Once again, I proved that God honors His Words above His name. We got back to Katmandu safely.

## The impartation of the gift of healing to the pastor's wife

The day before we left to return home, the wife of the pastor who was our chaperone met with us. She was not with us during the three-day conference, but the Holy Ghost was still upon us. While we were praying, I held her by the hand and prayed that God would use her for His glory, and that she will be able to lay her hands upon the sick and they shall recover. I spoke as the Holy Ghost gave me utterance, I told her that going forward whenever she places her hands on individuals it will bring deliverance and breakthrough in the name of Jesus. To God be the glory, the report has been great, she now travels with her husband walking in the prophetic of laying of hands. Those who needs healing, those who are possessed with demons/unclean spirit, and those who are struggling with depression and oppression are now being delivered because she now walks with the Grace that was released upon her.

Nepal is a place that I will never forget, because of the mighty outpouring power of the Holy Ghost and has now become one of our mission places. We supply them yearly with Bibles and other ministry gifts for the growth and the development of the ministry. God's power is not limited to a specific culture or geographic location. It is a transcendent force that operates beyond the confines of human constructs. God's omnipotent and omnipresent nature permeates every corner of the universe. His divine power is accessible to all individuals, irrespective of their cultural or religious affiliations.

# CHAPTER SEVEN
# UNITED STATES OF AMERICA

## THE GOD OF WONDERS, SIGNS AND MIRACLES!

*"God's divine power has given us everything we need for life and for godliness. This power was given to us through knowledge of the one who called us by his own glory and integrity." 2 Peter 1:3*

I believe that the Lord will do whatever it takes to bring us to the realm and level where He needs us to be so that our faith can grow from strength to strength. Every time I think that I have seen it all God will do yet another thing to remind me that He is still a wonder and a miracle working God. His word declares in *Isaiah 55:8-9*; **"My thoughts are not your thoughts, and my ways are not your ways, declares the Lord. Just as the heavens are higher than the earth, so my ways are higher than your ways, and my thoughts are higher than your thoughts."**

## CONNECTICUT

### An angel unaware

I was heading to work on the Merritt Parkway South bound. On this route it is very tricky, especially early mornings, because if there is an accident or any reason for traffic build up, you can be there for hours. The exits were far apart and so there is no way of getting off and on, and soft shoulders were nonexistent. That morning while driving, suddenly I saw on the dashboard a light flashing that looked like there was something wrong with the battery. Different lights kept flashing on the dashboard, and I felt like the car was slowing down. Before I could pull over to the side, the car came to a halt. I became very nervous and began to panic. Traffic was already backed up and I could hear the drivers blowing their horns and trying to get pass me.

I was not even close to an exit and out of nowhere a gentleman came up to my window. I was so afraid, he assured me that I will be fine and that he was going to push the car out of the road to allow the other cars to go around me. He also told me not to get out of the vehicle for any reason until either the police or the tow truck arrives. In my rear-view mirror I saw a white van, the man stepped away after he pushed my car to the side. I looked down to pick up my teacup to take a sip and then to wave my hand to say thank you but neither the man nor the white van was in sight. There was no way he could have passed me that fast because traffic was backed up. I could not believe what I had just experienced, I was astonished by that encounter but then I was reminded of *Hebrews 13:2, **"God will send an angel in the form of a person to help you in the time of need."*** The tow truck came, and everything worked out and I made it home safely.

## Healing of my rotator cuff and broken shoulder bone reattached

In 2021 during the height of the Covid-19 pandemic when the world was at a standstill of uncertainty. Everyone was concerned about their well-being; some days were very difficult for me, because I did not know if I was going to be one of the victims of this virus, that took out so many of our loved ones. One day while being outside I had a great fall. When I got up, I felt a very excruciating pain coming from my right shoulder, I could hardly keep my head up. I drove myself to the emergency room and upon arrival the doctor took one look and realized that I was in much pain. He sent me to do a couple tests which included an Xray, and after a couple hours the result of the Xray showed that my right shoulder was slipped out of the socket.

The doctor reassured me that he would give me a medication that would put me out for a couple minutes so that he could put my shoulder back in place. He stated that the severity of the pain would subside significantly once my shoulder was back in place. He gave me pain killers and told me he did not think I needed it, but I should use on a as needed basis. Well, I went home that night, and in the morning, I tried to turn and my Lord, my God, it seemed like something worst had happened to my right hand overnight. The pain was hitting me from the front of my shoulder, center of the shoulder, and the backside of my arm. In my heart I knew something was radically wrong.

I called the number that was on my discharge paperwork and told them what was happening to me. They referred me to a specialist who was kind enough to see me that same day. Everything was moving so fast. He requested for me to do an MRI and then placed my shoulder in a sling and told me to keep it in the sling until the MRI was completed and he got the results.

Strong pain medications were prescribed for me; one made me feel like I was going out of my mind and the other one made me so sleepy that I would sleep most of the day. It took three days before the MRI results were available. When I went in to get the results, as I sat and waited it felt like an eternity. When the doctor finally came, I knew something was wrong but not to the extreme it turned out to be. He told me that a piece of the bone was broken off from the socket that held the shoulder in place, and my rotator cuff was torn. His concern was not necessarily that of the torn rotator cuff but of the bone that was broken off and lodged in the back of my arm. He said that surgery was very much needed to repair the torn rotator cuff so that my right shoulder would not be dislocated like that again.

I went for a consultation and the day before surgery, I had to do another test to make sure that everything was ready for the procedure. This was routine pre operation procedures, but the saints were praying, and I was also praying and fasting. I remembered the Sunday before I went for the last set of tests, that morning when I got up, I felt like someone had a knife in my shoulder cutting into my skin. I told my sister in the Lord who was there assisting me to get dressed, that something was happening, but I could not explain it. I went to Church in pain, I preached the Word of God that day in pain with my hand in the sling. I was determined not to let satan win. I heard clearly while in the middle of the message that what happened to me was not for me to be ashamed, but that this would bring Him glory and honor. I told the saints what God had said, and He needed to show His people that He still works miracles not only in 2001, 2018, 2019 but also in 2021.

While preaching the Word I felt a sensation like fire, going through my hand. I continued to speak the Word of God and in that moment, I believed that God was performing another miracle on me. I came home that day and the scripture that came to mind was *2 Corinthians 12: 9*, **"So I will brag even the more about my weaknesses. In order that Christ's power will live in me. Therefore, I accept weakness, mistreatment, hardship, persecution, and difficulties suffered for Christ. It's clear that when I'm weak I'm strong."** My testimony and witness for God became even greater that day. Upon my return to the doctor that Tuesday, he walked in the room with my before and after tests, he said to me, "Mrs. Fuller there is no need for the procedure." I distinctly heard the doctor say, "something miraculous happened." The bone that was broken off had reattached itself into its rightful position and that all I needed was physical therapy. I began to give thanks right in the eyes of the doctor. All praise and glory belong to the Almighty God. He showed Himself mighty once again. Like He told Jeremiah **"I am the Lord God of all humanity. Nothing is too hard for me,"** *(Jeremiah 32:27)*. Today that arm is much stronger than my left arm that was not affected. To God be the glory!

## Lump in my breast

In 2009 three years after giving birth to my two amazing children (twin) Rachel and Isaiah. I went to do my routine mammogram and from the look of the technician's face I knew something was wrong. I thought to myself what the issue could be. The doctor came in and said that from the look of the ultrasound, he recognized that there was a lump in both of my breasts. He told me that I needed to do an MRI and a biopsy to know exactly what the conclusion of the findings were. He told me that I needed to do this right away. A part of me wanted to get angry with God, the "what if's", "what if I had cancer?", "what will happen to my children?", "what will happen to those who are depending on me," questions were heavy on my mind. In the middle of all my thoughts and questions, my spirit man woke up and began to take a stand.

I began to speak over myself with the word of God. I recited *Psalm 118:16 -17, "The right hand of the Lord displays strength, the right hand of the Lord is help high. The right hand of the Lord displays strength. I will not die. But I will live and tell what the Lord has done."* Because you are reading this book, I will proceed to tell you what the Lord has done. After I left the doctor's office, I went into three days of fasting and prayer without food or water. I set aside everything and went into deep conversation with God. I was instructed by the Holy Ghost to take from my prayer shawl two pieces of Tzitzit, which are the fringes that hung from the shawl. I was to put one in each bra during this time of seeking God for another miracle. Well, after the third day of being in the presence of Lord, I went back to the doctor to do my examination that they had recommended for me to do.

The technician began to do the ultrasound to target the lumps so that they could do the biopsy. Instantly a peace came over me, a sense of knowing that God is, and that He was about to show Himself mighty. By the look on the technician's face once again I knew that she saw something that confused her. The doctor himself came in and began to look for the lumps that they said they needed to do the biopsy on. He went to the left side, nothing. He went to the right, nothing. He took the probing device to go underneath my armpit to check, nothing. Miraculously, not only one of the lumps was gone but both were gone in Jesus' name. The doctor kept on saying look at this film Mrs. Fuller, there's nothing coming up. He said whatever I did I must continue to do it. I said to everyone that was present, that of myself I could have not done it. I shared and testified about the God of ALL grace. I let them know with all confidence that He does miracles and that He was ALL powerful and there was nothing that He cannot do. Job had this to say in *Job 5: 8-9*, ***"But I would seek God's help and present my case to him. He does great things that we cannot understand and miracles that we cannot count."*** Not only can He turn water into wine, heal the sick and raise the dead. I am living proof that He still does the impossible by removing those lumps/masses that were in my breast. This has caused my faith to increase and my passion to experience more in this realm have been heightened significantly.

## Co-worker healed from cancerous lumps in her neck

I hold this miracle very dear to my heart because of the circumstances surrounding it. My role at work was changed and so I had to be trained on the new role. Anyone who knows me, knows that when I introduce myself, I always use my name, and not any of the titles that are ascribed to me. I also believe that by your words and character you will be known. God does not make mistakes in anything that He does, and so when this new position was given, I knew that He was up to something extraordinary. When we can see things from God's perspective, things will fall into place much faster and easier so that the divine will of God can be fulfilled. My trainer was very good at what she does and went beyond her usual way of training to ensure that I was comfortable and gaining the knowledge I need to get my job done. I appreciated her so much because her attention to detail helped me greatly.

During our interaction she came to the knowledge that I was a believer in the God who works miracles and does ALL things well! I would consistently share with her the omnipotence of God. On several occasions she would request that I pray for her, and I did. On this day she called and from the tone of her voice I knew something was wrong with her. She told me that she had a few lumps in her neck and that she had already done an ultra-sound, however, her doctor was very concerned because of the size and where they were located. They now wanted her to do a biopsy. Upon hearing this report, I was neither nervous nor afraid, I told her with all confidence that God was going to work this one out for her. She hung up and I continued working, but because my heart was in a meditative position, the Lord told me to get my prayer shawl and I should let her use it for the next three days.

I was a bit nervous about the instructions I had received, but because I had seen God work, and I know His voice, I immediately picked up my phone and called her back. I shared with her the instructions that the Lord had given me and explained what the prayer shawl is and its use. She gladly accepted what I said. Before I left her, I prayed the prayer of faith. She wore my prayer shawl for three days and I continued to pray with her and for her. Upon arrival to do her scheduled biopsy, the technician did another ultra-sound to give them a better look in preparation for the biopsy. They asked her sit in a room, and she waited for a very long time. As the wait extended, she began to get nervous wondering what was taking them so long. She was assuming the worst because of the extensive wait.

She reported that the doctor came and stood at the door and said to her, "Ma'am I am not sure what has happened, but from what I am looking at and comparing to the previous ultrasound the lumps have magically disappeared." She asked him if he was looking at the correct results, and he said to her, the lumps are all gone and that there was no need to proceed with the scheduled biopsy. Miracles inspire hope, provide solace, and challenge the boundaries of human comprehension. This miracle along with others continue to captivate my imagination, reminding me of the existence of a reality beyond this material world. They leave me wanting to explore the depths of His power and anointing.

The act of using one's clothes as a point of contact is biblical. Incidents are recorded in *Acts 19:11-12*. Paul was doing extraordinary miracles by the power of God while in Ephesus. People would bring pieces of clothing, specifically handkerchiefs or aprons, to Paul so that they could be touched by him. This was done so that the sick and diseased could then touch the items and be healed or delivered from evil spirits.

It was not the physical cloth itself that held any power, but rather it was a point of contact or connection to the spiritual gifts and power that

God was working through Paul. Touching something associated with Paul's ministry activated faith for healing.

This was the case with my co − worker using my prayer shawl. Now she has been telling the good news that Jesus Christ is the same God yesterday, today, and forever. Her testimony of God's healing virtue, by following the instructions I gave her, and our collective faith in God has been a blessing to many and have helped to strengthen their faith.

## Depressed woman healed

*Jeremiah 32:27* states, **"I am the Lord God of all humanity. Nothing is too hard for me."** So many times, I have received phone calls and text messages to pray for individuals who are depressed, oppressed, those struggling with mental disorders, anxiety, and suicidal thoughts. Through prayers and faith in God I have received testimonies time and time again outlining the miraculous works of God. The grace that God has endowed in this area allows me to operate in the gifts of healing and deliverance. Like the Apostle Paul who states in *1 Corinthians 15:10*, **"But God's kindness made me what I am, and that kindness was not wasted on me. Instead, I worked harder than all the others. It was not I who did it, but God's kindness was with me."** I take no credit for anyone's deliverance it is all because of God's amazing grace.

I remembered so vividly a young lady came across my path. She was severely depressed and struggling with mental disorder due to the reality of losing a sibling that she was very close to. She had gotten to the place where she no longer prayed for herself. I strongly believe that whenever God put someone in your path it is for a reason, and we should ask ourselves the questions: what lesson is there for me to learn? what instructions are there for me to follow? Through the Holy Ghost and His direction, I knew that this young lady was not only struggling mentally but also spiritually. I knew that this case needed more than one session so that she could, accept and identify the different areas in her life that needed healing and deliverance. She needed to embrace the fact that the Lord can do all things and that He specializes in the impossibilities.

During one of our sessions the anger was so intense, the counselee demonstrated so much pain and she asked, "God, why did You let this bad thing happen to my family?" The Holy Ghost had me respond to her with the use of the Word of God in *Isaiah 57:1* ***"Righteous people die, and no one comes, loyal people are taken away and no one understands righteous people are spared when evil comes."*** Like a lightning bolt, the Word gave her consolation that her loved one had been spared and given eternal life and that He would be saved from the wrath to come. What a session it was I must agree that it had nothing to do with me but through the Word of God. ***"God's Word is living and active, it is sharper than any two-edged sword, and cuts as deep as the place where soul and spirit meet, the place where joints and marrow meets. God's word judges a person's thoughts and intentions. No creature can hide from God. Everything is uncovered and exposed for Him to see,*** (*Hebrews 4:12 – 13*).

Another scripture during the session that was relevant was *St. John 6:63,* ***"Life is spiritual. Your physical existence doesn't contribute to that life. The words that I have spoken to you was spiritual. They are life."*** As I explained the scripture to her, she was able to wrap her drained and exhausted mind around what I was saying. God began to manifest His strength in every area that needed healing and deliverance. Every time we met, I would allow the Holy Ghost to provide the directions, some sessions I allowed the counselee to let the tears flow without uttering a word, knowing that every tear that fell God knew what it meant. Other sessions, I had to speak with the power of the Holy Ghost and the authoritative grace of God over her life to take a stand. I declared that there would be no retreat, no surrender, and that she was not going back to the place of hurt, bitterness, anger, strife, and depression. The Holy Ghost ministered to her using me as a conduit to mend, comfort and restore the areas in her life that was broken.

In one of the sessions this individual shared with me that she was on medication for depression and anxiety. Now let me say this, I am not a license clinician, and I am not a psychologist but one thing I do know, is that I have the Holy Ghost that gives me the power to function where it is needed the most. So, in this session I began to declare the Word of the Lord according to *Philippians 4:8-9*, **"Finally, brothers and sisters, keep your thoughts on whatever is right or deserves praise; things that are true, honorable, fair, pure, acceptable, or commendable. Practice what you've learned and received from me, what you heard and saw me do. Then the God who gives this peace will be with you."** Once, I repeated the Word of God immediately I heard the voice of the Almighty God saying, this will be the last of the strong man that is holding this individual captive. The spirit of depression was broken, the spirit of anxiety was lifted, the spirit of fear, doubts, guilt, and of low self-esteem was broken. I lead this person in prayer as the Holy Ghost washed her body, soul, and spirit. What a remarkable transformation took place, this individual is now living her best life using the Word of God as the standard and being an asset to the body of Christ.

Rest assured, God not only can deliver you from any sickness, diseases, illnesses, and pain, but He can also deliver you from depression, oppression, anxiety, and whatever difficult situations we may face. *Joel 2:32* states, **"Then whoever calls on the name of the Lord will be saved. Those who escape will be on Mount Zion and in Jerusalem. Among the survivors will be those whom the Lord calls as the Lord has promised."** Whenever our God makes a promise, He will fulfill it. Not one of His words will return unto Him void, but it shall accomplish what it was sent out to do.

One of the keys for healing, deliverance, and restoration, is the use of the Word of God in every area of our lives. The Word of God possesses a profound power that transcends time, culture, and individual belief systems. The Word of God offers healing and restoration to the brokenhearted and weary. Its messages of love, forgiveness, and redemption provide comfort and hope to those who have experienced pain, loss, or despair. It encourages individuals to seek healing and restoration through faith, guiding them toward emotional and spiritual wholeness. It offers a balm for the wounded soul, fostering healing and the renewal of hope. You too can experience the supernatural power of His Word.


# MASSACHUSETTS

## Sick parishioner healed

*Proverbs 4: 21 – 22,* **"Do not lose sight of these things. Keep them deep within your heart, because they are life to those who find them, and they heal the whole body."** I was on a trip to minister the Word of God in Boston, Massachusetts. The saints were invited to come along with me. Most of the times they are unable to accompany me because of the distance of the assignments. However, Boston is only two and a half hours from Connecticut, so a few of the saints were extremely excited to be in this Women's and Men's conference. A sister from our local assembly was on this trip and upon arrival in Boston, it was brought to my attention she was in such pain, that they do not know if this woman could even get back to her home in Connecticut.

She sat through most of the service. When I got up and began to minister the Word of the Lord, I asked everyone to stand before I made the altar call. I said in the Spirit, those that are sick, those feeling good, or those not feeling good, everyone please stand. Through experience I knew that whenever God gives me specific instructions His miraculous power was going to be demonstrated. Through the obedience to the voice of God, I told everyone, in the hearing of my voice, that God has spoken and if they are believing God for a miracle they should step out in the aisle. I told them to place their hand wherever the sickness, pain, or condition existed. Like fire, the Holy Ghost descended and the parishioner that could hardly walk to go into the sanctuary, and did not move during the service, began to leap and shout thanking God that she was healed.

She testified that she felt a liquid running down her back once I began to declare healing in the atmosphere. To be crystal clear that the pain was gone she bent forward, backward, sideways and lifted her hands above her head. There was no pain and no discomfort, the back pain that she had was caused from a previous injury that she had gotten some years ago. That night, God healed her and gave her a testimony so she can speak of His goodness. The other parishioners that were on the trip heard her cry in the car and observed her in the service, and in that moment, they had an opportunity to witness the healing power of God. *Malachi 4:2* states, ***"The Sun of Righteousness will rise with healing in his wings for you people who fear my name. You will go out and leap like calves let out of a stall."*** That scripture became a reality as those that travelled with her began to leap and praise the Lord.

Something to keep in our minds is that we should always be open to the unexpected. When it comes to God and the things of God, we must always have the spirit of great expectation. The spirit of expectation is a powerful state of mind and heart characterized by hope, anticipation, and a belief in the fulfillment of desired outcomes. It is a mindset that looks beyond current circumstances and embraces the possibility of positive change and blessings. The spirit of expectation opens the door to miracles in our lives. When we expect positive outcomes and hold a state of anticipation, we become more attuned to opportunities, and unexpected blessings. Let us trust God for the impossible.

## NEW JERSEY

### Unprecedented outpouring

I am continually amazed at the ways in which God chooses to make His presence known. Many years ago, when I was serving as an assistant pastor, I was invited to preach at a Women's Conference. I could sense the presence of the Lord and feel the brush of angel's wings in the congregation. As I stood behind the sacred desk, I shared what God had given me for His people. I remember leaving the rostrum and walking down to the main floor with my handkerchief in hand. Suddenly I threw my handkerchief to the right side and like an ocean wave, everyone on that side fell backwards in worship. A lady who was tarrying for the Holy Ghost, received the gift of the Holy Ghost in that moment, with the evidence of speaking in tongues. This was one moment when I recognized the magnitude of the grace of God over my life.

## My personal divine encounter

It was in the winter season in the month of February, when potential snow or ice fall can make it treacherous for travelling. I was asked to minister at an assembly in Orange, New Jersey, affectionately called, "Sweet Orange" by the parishioners. I was previously asked to minister at the same assembly before, but upon instruction from the Lord, I was told it was not my time to be there. I gladly embraced the decision to decline the invite. One year to that date, I was asked again to open their Men's and Women's conference, this time I accepted the invitation. The week leading up to the assignment I sought the Lord. He gave me the word to share with His people.

The day that I was scheduled to minister a huge snowstorm hit my town in Connecticut! I had to get help to dig out the church bus so that we could go on this assignment. While New Jersey did not get much snow, Connecticut had thirteen inches of snow. God began to do what He does best by selecting the individuals assigned to be with me. Despite the hard labor of digging out the van and the inclement weather we were excited and ready to meet our brothers and sisters from another state. We sang and praised God during our one hour and forty-five minutes ride. We parked the bus, and everyone was eager to go into the service. As soon as I entered the main entrance of the building and made my way to the right inside of the lobby, I heard a distinct voice like an amplified microphone saying, "THIS NIGHT YOUR MINISTRY WILL BE ESTABLISHED." I looked to see what direction the voice was coming from and turned to the person that was next to me to ask them if they heard what I just heard. The Spirit within me said this was not for them, but for me. I was quickly escorted by the person who was assigned to be my armor bearer for the night. It was the first night of the conference and from experience and custom the first night for any gathering was usually not as supported as the other nights that followed. I was not looking for many saints and of course a conference normally opens with a speaker that may be new to the ministry or not well known.

The memory of that night still stays with me, the house was full! Like the day of Pentecost everyone was in one place, and in my heart I prayed for the one accord. I thought to myself if I had gotten the opportunity to change my mind last minute I would because of what I saw. I was placed next to the Bishop's wife, which I can proudly say this same ministry is now the organization that I serve as the first woman Overseer for the island of Antigua. That night the Co-Pastor of the Church introduced me with such high distinction that I said to myself who is this person she is talking about. Upon receiving the microphone, I took the steps to the podium by faith. I began to do protocol by acknowledging the Presiding Bishop and everyone in their rightful position. I began with the song, "Blessed Jesus hold my hand yes, I need thee every hour thru this land, this pilgrim land, protect me by the saving power. Hear my plea, my feeble plea, oh dear Lord look down on me when I kneel in prayer blessed Jesus hold my hand."

Immediately the Lord showed up once again, like a domino effect, everyone fell on their faces and for two and a half hours everyone was laid flat in the presence of the Lord. That night was one where heaven and earth met. I saw God in all His glory; angelic beings were all over the building, ascending and descending. I heard the voice of God in *Psalm 62:11,* **"God has spoken once. I heard it said twice; power belongs to God."** The very line that I heard echoed when I first walked in the building was being echoed in my ear repeatedly: "THIS NIGHT YOUR MINISTRY WILL BE ESTABLISHED."

That night went down in history, the Lord used me to be a great blessing. At the end of the service some were saying that they had never experienced such glory in the house of Lord. Others stated that everything about me had changed; one of the ladies that came with us on the bus shared that even my face glowed like a bright light was shining from me. I remember her pinching me and saying she wanted to make sure that I was back on earth. She was in awe to see the glory of God that was in the house and how mightily the Lord had used me.

From that night until this very hour God did exactly what He said He would do. The doors were swung open for me to travel to different parts of the world; Jamaica, Canada, Nepal, Israel, most of the Islands, and many of the States of America. Better yet the grace of God over my life has become stronger, richer, and the overflow is more evident in each service or place that I go to minister.

The more the miracles, signs, and confirmations occurred, the more I became hungry and thirsty for more of Him. I needed more of His grace and His anointing and so I surrendered to Him and asked Him to use me for His glory. I told Him I wanted ALL of Him and none of me. I came to realize that if there was even a little of me, then I would run the risk of not experiencing all of His Glory! I noticed that the more I stepped in the prophetic, the more the challenges came. But the sweetness of His Shekinah Glory was more satisfying than the troubles or the setbacks that I would experience. I would never trade this position of privilege for the wealth and riches that this world has to offer. To experience this kind of glory one must be dead to self and submit to the divine order of God for their life. It is not sufficient to only hear His voice, but it is submitting to that which He Hath called us to do. This is the winning formula that has allowed me to continue to fulfill my purpose and destiny in God.

## Woman healed from stage three kidney disease and osteoporosis

I was given an assignment to minister the Word of God during a Holy Convocation. As always, I sought the Lord for a word for His people. I never depend on my own strength or intellect. I knew that if I wanted the Lord to move, I had to make Him the center of all that I do and depend only on Him. I have asked the Lord so often to confirm HIS WORD, not for self-gratification but rather as a reminder for me that He will never leave or forsake me.

The testimony I am about to share occurred in 2019 but I was only made aware of this in 2023 while ministering at a Women's Retreat. I was among a group of ladies, many of which I have never seen before. On the Friday night, individuals were sharing their personal testimonies, fears, and pain. This older lady got up and reminded me how I saved her life. I had no recollection of this woman; however, she shared that while I was ministering the Word, I came off the platform, went over to where she was sitting and pointed directly in her forehead. I told her she shall not die; but she shall live to declare the glory of the Lord.

She stated that the following week she went and saw a doctor because of the things she was experiencing. She was diagnosed with Stage 3 kidney disease and osteoporosis. The mother stated that she was shocked but not worried because she recalled that night the power of the Holy Ghost came down upon her and she knew something miraculous was done in her body. Four years later she is still rejoicing and boasting about the healing she received that night. Her kidneys are good and no trace of osteoporosis. These signs shall follow them that believe, and He will not go back upon His Word.

## Infilling of the Holy Ghost and viral video that continues to provide deliverance

April 2023, I was invited to my headquarters Church to minister the Word of God during our 38th Church Anniversary Service. Upon ministering the Word of the Lord, I made it clear that coming to my headquarters church was not just an invitation to another service but a place where I can be refueled and experience an open heaven. That night was amazing! It began with a family of five that was baptized five days prior to me getting there. The number five in biblical numerology represents God's grace, mercy, and favor. As I walked down the aisle, I threw my handkerchief on one of the ladies from that family and instantaneously, she was filled with the Holy Ghost with the evidence of speaking in the heavenly language. The recording for that night went viral. Individuals from all walks of life were commenting even eight weeks later, that by listening and watching the video they too were experiencing deliverance from demons, the spirit of depression and anxiety, and so many were restored with physical strength from the God of all Grace. Each experience has left me in amazement, and I am very humbled that God has selected and trust me with this level of grace to be used by Him. *https://tinyurl.com/HolyGhostPower2023*

## NEW YORK

### *Charge of negligence manslaughter dropped*

New York is one of my favorite states in the United States of America. It is said to be where it happens, and it truly happened in New York. It is said that this state is full of wickedness and evil, but God's presence is sovereign and is always at work. I remember being the facilitator at a Women's Retreat where the Lord directed me to one of the ladies. As I walked towards her the Lord instructed me to tell her that He was going to show her how powerful He is and that every charge against her will be dropped. Oh my God! When I delivered the message, the Holy Ghost began to move on her and the saints that heard what was just said in the atmosphere began to praise God. They were praising God for the Word of knowledge that was uttered knowing that God still uses individuals to bring comfort and assurance to the hurting. After that prophetic word was shared, the woman confirmed that she was charged with negligence manslaughter.

After many months of deliberation and court appearances, she became fearful, frustrated, and began losing hope in the word that I had spoken over her life. I assured her to keep the faith and not to give up. I reminded her according to the Word of God found is *Psalm 19:9,* **"The fear of the Lord is pure, it endures forever. The decisions of the Lord are true. They are completely fair."** I comforted her with the Word of God, which was all I had, knowing that my words were not sufficient. The Lord according to His Word, delivered her from all charges. What a testimony she had! Once again God showed Himself mighty.

## Woman healed from excruciating pain

Once again, I was given the opportunity to serve in a Women's retreat. One of my niches for the Body of Christ is serving in retreats for women, youth, and the entire family. On this occasion while teaching a session on healing and deliverance, I experienced a sharp, excruciating pain coming from the back of my head going down my neck. Immediately, I thought to myself that I was having a stroke, but then my spiritual antenna went up. The teaching I was engaged in caused me to pull someone else's sickness. I stopped in the middle of the teaching and explained to the group what I was feeling. I stated that someone in the room right now is experiencing much pain and I prayed the prayer of faith.

A young lady stood up and indicated that she was the one having the pain from the back of her head, and once the prayer of faith was said the pain was gone and she was healed. *James 5:15,* **"Prayers offered in faith will save those who are sick, and the Lord will cure them. If you have sinned, you will be forgiven."** The prayer of faith is rooted in unwavering belief, trust, and confidence in the divine. It goes beyond mere words and rituals, encompassing a profound conviction that the divine is present, listening, and capable of responding to the sincere pleas of the faithful. The young woman still speaks on this instant miracle to those she meets, sharing that God is truly amazing and that He will do exactly what He said according to His Word.

## Phone shattered in pieces

In our life we all struggle to do right. The Apostle Paul in his writing to the Romans stated in *Romans 7: 18-19,* **"I know that nothing good lives in me; that is nothing good like, in my corrupt nature. Although I have the desire to do it. I don't do the good I want to do. Instead, I do the evil that I don't want to do. In other words, I do things that even when instructed don't do it because, of being disobedient or even not trusting to what God is doing."** God at times uses our stubborn, self-reluctant, disobedient ways to show that He is always in control. On this assignment the Lord instructed me to tell the group that in order for them to receive from the Lord, they should put away their electronic devices to focus on being in the presence of the Lord. I further stated that no one should go home the same way they came.

After that night session, I was on my way to my room when I saw a group of young ladies talking. To get to my room I had to pass by them. In doing so I saw everyone with their cell phones in their hands. One of the young ladies said to me, "Pastor Fuller, I do not see the need for me to put away my cell phone, and I am telling you in your face that I will not be putting away mine." With the word of knowledge that I am graced with I said to this young woman according to *1 Samuel 15:22, "To follow instruction is better than to sacrifice."* She said once again, it does not take all of that to receive her blessing. I turned to her and said be it unto you; as I turned and stepped off no exaggeration, it was like a tornado passed through the hallway. The phone she had in her hand went flying, it fell onto the floor and could not be recognized. It was shattered and could not be repaired.

This was the proof she needed, and those that stood around her saw that when God needs your attention, He will send direct instructions for you to follow. Disobedience to God comes with a high cost, affecting individuals spiritually, morally, and practically. All the ladies that were standing and saw what happened, were in amazement to see what had just occurred and now stood in such great fear of how God works. For the remainder of that assignment the power of God manifested itself in a mighty and life changing way. The ladies received double portions of His anointing, breakthroughs, and deliverance. Some had a new and fresh outlook concerning their spiritual walk with the Lord. Today, that same young lady is one of my mentees with a desire to make God's instructions the blueprint for her life.

Even now this divine encounter still leaves me in bewilderment because there was no wind, no windows, no open doors to cause such a wind to have blown her phone out of her hand. Disobedience to God hinders personal growth and deprives individuals of blessings and opportunities.

Divine commands and guidance are intended to lead individuals towards their highest potential and purpose. By disregarding God's instructions, individuals may miss out on valuable lessons, personal development, and the fulfillment of their true potential. Disobedience closes doors to blessings, as individuals distance themselves from the divine favor and guidance that could have enriched their lives.

## God's will trumps ours

The concept of the will of the Lord, encompasses the belief that there is a divine plan and purpose that directs the course of human existence. It represents the idea that there is a higher power at work, guiding individuals and shaping the events according to His divine wisdom and providence. The Lord moves in mysterious ways to perform His wonders. I was visiting with an assembly that was having a conference, I was not the designated preacher. I was there for fellowship and support. The God I serve is very purposeful, deliberate, and intentional. He will do whatever, whenever, however, He wants to do, so that His people can be healed delivered and set free. The pastor called on me to greet the congregation. Wow! What can I say, again God showed up for His people. The moment I stood in the pulpit the power of the Holy Ghost came down upon me and I began to speak as the Holy Ghost gave me the unction.

The people were stirred in their hearts and there was a shift in the atmosphere. I stepped back to my seat and the Pastor tried to quiet everyone so that He could introduce the speaker who had flown into New York as the guest preacher. When he finally got an opportunity to make the introduction and the guest preacher stood up and took the microphone, he made it clear that he may be slow when it comes to being street smart, but was very sensitive on the move of God. He stated that although on the advertisement he was the assigned preacher, God was doing something in His house.

He apologized to the host pastor and respectfully asked him to allow me to finish what God hath started. The measure of grace that was upon my life allowed me to preach like never before. Souls were challenged to surrender their lives to God, believers were moved to tap in the realm of the Spirit to reposition themselves and come in full alignment with God's plan and purpose for their lives. Many that were sick began to take the sweat that was falling from my forehead and rubbing it wherever they were experiencing any kind of sickness, disease, pains, or any discomfort in their bodies.

God was moving heavily in the service, and this brought about a spirit of conviction to those who did not believe in the supernatural power of God. God sat upon His people like the Day of Pentecost. When I was through ministering to the people of God that's when I began replaying what just happened in the service. Surrendering to the will of God allows us to cultivate a sense of inner peace and serenity, even amidst criticism and uncertainty. At the end of the service, I was given clothes to change into that were three times my size because my outfit was soaking wet with sweat. The wisdom of God surpasses human comprehension and transcends the limitations of our mortal existence. May we humbly open ourselves to the wisdom of God, allowing it to shape our thoughts, guide our actions, and lead us towards a life of purpose, fulfillment, and deep spiritual connection.

## Lady delivered from abominable lifestyle

Not by might, not by power, but my Spirit says the Lord. This one I remembered because this was at a Youth Retreat where there were so many young people. Innately I love to be around the youths. It was in the early morning prayer meeting which I consider to be the first fruit one gives to the Lord. The auditorium was filled with young people crying out to the Lord. I laid flat on my face doing the same thing, the Lord began to show me a young lady that was living a lifestyle that He despised. The enemy had told her lies that she was no good, and that she would never amount to anything.

Once I got off my knees the Lord sent me directly to the young lady. She was crying out for help, but the satanic stronghold was blocking and holding her hostage to this kind of behavior. I placed my hand around her and said to her, "You know that God loves you? She responded, "God loves everyone!" I asked her if she knew that He cares and wants to use her for His glory. She stated that God does not even care for her, and she was ready to go home. She was very firm when she said, "nothing I said at this point would change anything." I knew for sure that the spirit that held her captive was fierce and would not readily go. I needed God to give me specific details so when I opened my mouth to speak to this young woman, she would recognize that it was God Himself. I was embolden by *Jeremiah 1:5* which states, ***"Before I formed you in the womb, I knew you, before you were born I set you apart for my holy purpose. I appointed you to be a prophet to the nations."*** My spirit man was now sensitive and ready to say exactly what the Lord needed me to do and speak.

So once again the Lord told me to remind her that He loves her and that He is here to deliver her from that lifestyle. She turned and looked directly and fiercely into my eyes and said, "I am not doing anything." Now the Lord spoke once again and said to tell her that the under garment she is wearing was purchased by the individual that she was involved with. The Lord also gave me the color of the underwear. She began to scream, a few of the Youth Directors and myself took her to another room, where I walked her through the process of deliverance. I prayed the prayer of deliverance and through the power of the Holy Ghost, she made a declaration of affirmation that from this day forward she was not going back to that lifestyle.

One thing that stood out for me during this deliverance process was that she took out her phone and factory reset it, because she wanted a fresh start. The scripture came to my remembrance concerning being delivered from ungodly lifestyle, *Philippians 3:18-21*, ***"I have often told you and now tell you with tears in my eyes, that many live as the enemies of the Cross of Christ. In the end they will be destroyed. Their own emotions are their god, and they take pride in the shameful things they do. Their minds are set on worldly things. We however are citizens of heaven; we look forward to the Lord coming from heaven as our savior.***

**Through His power to bring everything under His authority, He will change our humble bodies and make them like His glorified body."** This young woman needed a change; a change of mind, heart, soul, and spirit and so she took back her faith and walk with God. She began to praise God, she shared with us that she felt like a brand-new person.

Like Moses when He came from off Mount Sinai, his face was glowing you could tell he had encountered the Lord. The glory of the Lord was shining on and around her. The power of God holds a unique capability to bring about transformative change in our lives. The power of God facilitates a renewal of the mind and heart, transforming negative thought patterns, destructive beliefs, and unhealthy desires. Through prayer, meditation, and the study of scriptures, individuals gain spiritual insight and wisdom, aligning their thoughts and attitudes with God's divine truth. This process of renewal leads to a shift in perspective, fostering a positive mindset, a heart filled with love, and a desire to please God.

# CHAPTER EIGHT

## WE ALL CAN BE GRACED TO BE AN INSTRUMENT FOR HIM

*"It is God who produces in you the desires and actions that please him." - Philippians 2:13.*

Throughout history, mankind has sought solace, guidance, and hope in the divinity of Christ. For countless individuals, the belief in God serves as a beacon of faith, and with it comes the hope for miracles. Miracles, often defined as extraordinary events that defy natural explanations, have been the subject of awe and wonder for centuries. Miracles act as profound testimonies to the existence and benevolence of God. They stand as undeniable evidence that there is a force beyond the realm of human comprehension, capable of defying natural laws and bringing about extraordinary change. Miracles manifest in various forms, whether it be physical healing, restored relationships, financial provisions, or even unexplainable coincidences. Each miracle serves as a reminder of God's limitless power and His active involvement in the lives of His followers.

"These Signs Shall Follow Them That Believe ~ Graced To Be An Instrument For Him," documents miracles and divine encounters that occurred in this 21st century. This lends proof to the fact that if we believe, we too can experience miracles and divine encounters. To have these supernatural encounters one must:

- Put their faith in action
- Use prayer and meditation as a catalyst
- Challenge doubts
- Follow the instructions given by God

- Death to self
- Keep your heart in a meditative position

At the core of believing in God for miracles lies unwavering faith. Faith is an intangible force that transcends human understanding, enabling individuals to trust in the divine and its ability to manifest supernatural occurrences. Faith instills hope in the hearts of believers, assuring them that even the most daunting circumstances can be overcome through divine intervention. It is this profound trust in God's power and goodness that fuels the belief in miracles. The Bible states that he that comes to God must believe that He is and that He is a rewarder of them that seek Him. (Hebrews 11:6). We must step out in faith to receive from the Lord. Act on the beliefs and convictions of your faith, even when it feels uncomfortable or uncertain. Take steps of obedience that align with your understanding of God's will. Trust that God will provide the strength, resources, and guidance you need as you step out in faith. At times I had to trust Him when I could not trace Him and believe Him because He is God, and He never fails.

Prayer serves as a powerful conduit between humanity and the divine. It is an act of surrendering our individual will to a higher power, seeking guidance, strength, and intervention. As believers we often turn to prayer to communicate our desires, hopes, and pleas for miracles. Through prayer, one's faith is expressed and strengthened, creating a spiritual connection that allows believers to experience the transformative power of miracles. Meditation facilitates intimacy with God, spiritual insight, inner renewal, divine guidance, and Christlike character. It is a vital spiritual discipline in the life of a believer especially for those who desire to have more of God. In meditation, we listen for the gentle promptings and stirrings of Holy Ghost speaking into our lives and giving us specific instructions. I practice the discipline of meditation throughout my day, by ensuring that my heart remains in a meditative position no matter what is going on around me. This is a learned behavior and with daily practice it can be accomplished.

While the belief in God for miracles is a profound and empowering force, it is not immune to challenges and doubts. Skepticism and questioning are natural aspects of the human experience, and believers may grapple with moments of uncertainty. At times when ministering I am faced with those that do not believe the instructions that I am providing from God. Some would blatantly defy what I am saying, but in moments like these I must hold on to what I heard from the Holy Ghost. The enemy will play with our minds to make us second guess what we heard but we must be sensitive to the voice of God. However, it is through these challenges that faith is refined and strengthened. The stories of doubt for me in all instances have turned out to be unwavering conviction when the power of God is being manifested. Be resilient in your faith so that you too can have divine encounters and experience His miraculous power.

If we are going to have the experience of being used as an instrument or conduit for God, we must follow His instructions. Jesus had to follow His father's command when He walked on earth. When He was in the garden of Gethsemane and being faced with death, not my will but thine was His conclusion. He had to do what He came on earth to do as painful as it was. God, in His infinite wisdom and love will provide us with divine instructions as it relate to each encounter. As vessels set a part to be used by Him, it is important that we fully commit to following these instructions. Although, doing so can be challenging at times, the benefits of adhering to these instructions will produce the results we are looking for. As we walk in faithful obedience, we will receive the sweet fruits of His promises. Blind eyes will be opened; sick can be healed; lame walk; the dumb speak to name a few. There is no telling what He will do when we make His instructions priority and not trying to do things our way.

The call to "die to self" to be a vessel that God can use to perform miracles and experience divine encounters is not an easy path, but it is a path that leads to profound transformation and eternal rewards. It requires surrendering our own will, embracing selflessness, and crucifying our sinful nature. Through this process, we experience the abundant life that Christ promises, reflecting His love and grace to the world. The death to self is not a one-time event but a continuous process of transformation. It involves the renewing of our minds, aligning our thoughts, attitudes, and actions with the teachings of Christ. Through self-examination, repentance, and reliance on God's grace, we are transformed into His likeness, reflecting His character in our daily lives. It is then that God can use us to be a blessing to others because it is no longer you that lives but Christ that lives in you. It is here that we can see the miracles, signs, and wonders because now God can trust us with His grace knowing that He will get the glory out of our life.

Believing in God for miracles has a transformative impact on individuals and communities. Miracles have the power to restore faith in the face of adversity, renew hope in times of despair, and inspire acts of gratitude and compassion. Witnessing or experiencing a miracle ignites a deep sense of awe and wonder, instilling a lasting imprint on one's spiritual journey. Miracles not only strengthen the faith of the recipient but also serve as a source of inspiration for others, encouraging them to trust in God and believe that miracles are possible in their own lives. May you always remember that these signs follow them that believe!

# STRATEGIES FOR BUILDING ONE'S FAITH

*"Ask, and you will receive. Search, and you will find. Knock, and the door will be opened for you. - St. Matthew 7:7*

**Seek Knowledge:** Invest time in studying and deepening your understanding of your faith. Set aside time to read the scripture, if only a few verses or a chapter a day. Reading the Bible regularly exposes you to more of God's truth.
*Proverbs 2:6; Ephesians 1:17 & Proverbs 15:14.*

**Prayer and Meditation:** Establish a regular practice of prayer and meditation to develop a deeper connection with God. Set aside time each day to communicate with and listen to God. Prayer and meditation can help quiet the mind, cultivate inner peace, and open yourself to spiritual experiences.
*Colossians 3:2; Psalm 104:34; Psalm 19:14 & 1 Thessalonians 5:17.*

**Surround Yourself with a Faith Community:** Connect with a community of like-minded individuals who share your faith. Participate in religious services, join study groups, or engage in community activities. Being part of a faith community provides support, encouragement, and opportunities for learning and growth.
*Proverbs 13:20; 1 Corinthians 15:33; Proverbs 27:17 & Romans 12:16.*

**Reflect and Journal:** Take time for self-reflection and introspection. Journaling can be a helpful practice to express your thoughts, feelings, and experiences related to your faith. Reflecting on your spiritual journey, challenges, and moments of growth can deepen your understanding and strengthen your faith.
*Philippians 4:8; Isaiah 30:8 & Jeremiah 30:2.*

**Practice Gratitude:** Cultivate an attitude of gratitude by regularly acknowledging and appreciating the blessings in your life. Recognize the presence of God in everyday experiences and express gratitude for the gifts you have been given. Gratitude can foster a sense of contentment, trust, and connection with God.
*Psalm 107:1; Ephesians 5:20 & Colossians 3:17.*

**Engage in Service:** Actively seek opportunities to serve others and make a positive difference in the world. Practice acts of kindness, compassion, and generosity in alignment with your faith values. Serving others not only reflects your faith in action but also deepens your spiritual connection and strengthens your faith.
*Colossians 3:23- 24; 1 Peter 4:10 -11 & 1 Corinthians 3:5.*

**Embrace Doubts and Questions:** It is natural to have doubts and questions along your faith journey. Instead of suppressing or dismissing them, embrace them as opportunities for growth. Seek answers through study, reflection, and engaging in conversations with trusted mentors or spiritual leaders. Embracing doubt with an open mind can lead to a stronger, and a more resilient faith.
*James 1:5; Isaiah 41:10 & 13 & Proverbs 3:5-6.*

**Cultivate Mindfulness:** Practice being fully present in the moment, observing and appreciating the beauty and wonder of life around you. Mindfulness can help you deepen your connection with God by fostering a sense of awe, gratitude, and awareness of the presence of God in everyday experiences.
*Joshua 1:8; Psalm 77:11 -12 & Psalm 19:14*

**Continually re-commit your life to Christ:** Regularly considering areas of spiritual growth and re-dedicating your life to God keeps faith renewed.
*1 Kings 8:61;1 Peter 2:2; & Romans 12:1.*

**Listen to spiritual songs, psalms and hymns:** Uplifting songs and hymns of adoration can spark feeling and passion for God.
*Ephesians 5:19; Colossians 3:16 & Psalm 150.*

# REFLECTIONS

Write a list of requests that you are believing God for yourself or someone else.

_____

_____

_____

_____

_____

_____

How are you approaching God concerning these requests?

_____

_____

_____

_____

_____

What are some of the barriers/hinderances that could prevent one from having their request/s granted?

_____

_____

_____

_____

_____

How do you identify answered prayers?

_____

_____

_____

_____

_____

_____


Document the answers to your prayers!

_____

_____

_____

_____

_____

_____

# PASTOR OVERSEER
# MARY DANIEL-FULLER

Pastor ~ Overseer ~ Preacher ~ Retreat Facilitator ~
Teacher ~ Worship Leader ~ Author

Called as an Evangelist, serving as a Pastor, and appointed as an Overseer, **Pastor Mary Daniel-Fuller**, a native of Kingston, Jamaica is the seventh of ten children born to Albert and Ruby Daniel. At a tender age of twelve years old, Mary was baptized and within 672 hours she received the gift of the Holy Ghost at the Rehoboth Apostolic Church under the leadership of Pastor M. Bailey & Bishop B.S.E Dyer. It was from that moment Mary found herself stepping out on childlike faith into the mysteries of God.

Through the years Pastor Fuller has been graced to serve the Body of Christ in numerous capacities such as Missionary, Evangelist, Psalmist, Adjutant, Choir Director, International Women's President, Sunday School Teacher, and Youth President. While attending a February 2013 service in Orange, New Jersey, Pastor Fuller distinctly heard the voice of God say: **"Tonight is the night I will establish your Ministry."** That establishment and favor with God has transported her around the globe to preach the gospel in the United States, Canada, England, Jamaica, Barbados, Nepal, Antigua, and Grand Cayman. She also had the privilege of traveling to Israel where she baptized seven souls in river Jordan. Led by God, Pastor Fuller stepped out on faith in 2018 to pioneer and pastor the New Apostolic International Ministries (N-AIM) of Stratford, Connecticut. N-AIM is a vibrant congregation where everyone can be someone in Christ Jesus. In June 2023 Pastor Fuller was installed as Overseer of the 2nd Episcopal Diocese of Antigua for the Acts United Church International under the leadership of Bishop Lloyd Faulknor.

A key component of Pastor Fuller's ministry is that she believes her triumphs as well as every obstacle, barrier and challenge are an opportunity for God to show forth His mighty works. Her mantra, "I just want to serve the people of God," emboldens her to use the wisdom gleaned from her experiences to be a trusted prophetic voice to mentees, Pastors, Leaders, and others she encounters throughout her ministry. Her drive, ambitions, passion, and benevolence, stretches and motivates others to accept who they are in Christ cultivating gifts and talents to the glory of God.

Pastor Overseer Fuller can be contacted via email: lalisefuller@gmail.com or via her ministry Facebook page Mary Daniel-Fuller.

Printed in the United States
by Baker & Taylor Publisher Services